PRAISE FOR *THE GENIUS UNDER*

★ "Warm and wonderfully illustrated. . . . This humorous, informative, and engaging memoir will keep readers entertained." —*Booklist* (starred review)

★ "Yelchin, wonderfully, allows his text and pictures to interrupt each other with glee, reminding us how life begets art. It certainly does here." —*The Horn Book* (starred review)

★ "Yelchin's line drawings, re-created from his childhood sketches under the table, punctuate his story with visual humor and pathos. . . . Humorous, heartbreaking, and ultimately hopeful." —*Kirkus Reviews* (starred review)

★ "An unforgettable portrayal of one family's experiences living in the Soviet Union. . . . Captivating." —*School Library Journal* (starred review)

★ "A frank, engaging memoir. . . . At once comical and disquieting." —*Publishers Weekly* (starred review)

★ "Paints a vivid picture of life under the Soviet regime. . . . Energetic and often humorous amid the danger and tragedy." —*Bulletin of the Center for Children's Books* (starred review)

"A beautiful, layered memoir about how people thrive when their country is doing its best to stifle their dreams." —*Minneapolis Star Tribune*

"An idiosyncratic illustrated memoir of boyhood . . . that manages to amuse with its quirky details and disturb with the broad picture it paints of life under communism." —*The Wall Street Journal*

"An extraordinary work of memory told with clear-sightedness and ironic good humor, both disguising a great deal of pathos. This book is a recipe for survival for us all in a world growing tougher by the day." —David Small, winner of the Caldecott Medal and National Book Award Finalist for *Stitches*

"I read Eugene Yelchin's sad, funny memoir with tears and laughter. It is told with such exquisite humor and illustrated with such wonderful, biting drawings that, in spite of its darkness, I savored every word and every picture. A treat." —Uri Shulevitz, winner of the Caldecott Medal and three Caldecott Honors

THE
GENIUS
UNDER THE
TABLE

GROWING UP BEHIND THE IRON CURTAIN

EUGENE YELCHIN

CANDLEWICK PRESS

First paperback edition 2024

Library of Congress Catalog Card Number 2021945706
ISBN 978-1-5362-1552-6 (hardcover)
ISBN 978-1-5362-3624-8 (paperback)

24 25 26 27 28 29 SHD 10 9 8 7 6 5 4 3 2 1

Printed in Chelsea, MI, USA

This book was typeset in Tryst.
The illustrations were done in graphite.

Candlewick Press
99 Dover Street
Somerville, Massachusetts 02144

www.candlewick.com

A JUNIOR LIBRARY GUILD SELECTION

For my brother

THE FIRST TIME

I saw real American tourists, they hopped out of a tourist bus in Red Square in Moscow and cut in front of us in line.

"Nice manners!" my mother shouted. "We've been freezing our butts off for hours and they just breeze in like that?"

We were in line to the mausoleum where the founder of our country, Vladimir I. Lenin, was laid out embalmed like an Egyptian mummy. To see him, you had to wait your turn.

Making noise near Lenin's mausoleum was forbidden, but the Americans laughed and spoke in loud voices. The Americans and my mother were breaking the rules.

Everyone in line was staring at my mom for shouting, but I was staring at the Americans. The Americans' clothes were in vibrant colors I did not know existed. They did not fit in Red Square at all. The square may be called Red, but it is black and white in the winter. Most citizens in line were also dressed in black and white. Other colors were brown, army green, navy blue, and the red of our country's banner, flapping above the mausoleum.

Those were the colors of the Soviet rainbow.

My family had come to Moscow to watch my older brother, Victor, compete in a figure-skating

competition, but Dad said that it was our patriotic duty to see Lenin's mummy first. No one in the long line was allowed to complain. Except for my mother, of course.

"What are you complaining about, citizen?" the security guard whispered to Mom. He looked nervous that she was making a scene in the most sacred place in our country.

"Complaining?" my mother shouted. "You didn't hear me complaining yet, young man! I demand to know your name and rank! Write it down, Victor. Who's in charge around here?"

At last the line began to move, and Mom, having let off a little steam, became perfectly calm. She took my hand and we stepped into the mausoleum by the rules, in silence.

3

The mausoleum was spooky inside. The stone walls reflected no light, and what light could they reflect? There was not a single light bulb anywhere. I rose on my tiptoes, hoping to glimpse the American colors up ahead, but a citizen's back blocked my view.

The guards hurried us along the platform on which Lenin lay. I had never seen a dead person before, and this one had been dead since before I was born.

"Don't be scared, Yevgeny," Dad whispered to me. "You love Grandfather Lenin."

Lenin was grandfather to all Soviet children, which was

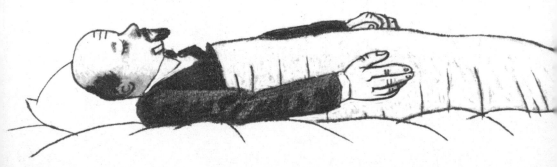

a little confusing. So many children in our country! How could all of us have the same grandfather? I did not know, but it was better not to ask. Asking questions was considered not patriotic.

I was six years old, and it was my first trip to the capital. While waiting in line I had been looking forward to seeing Lenin's mummy, but with these vibrant Americans nearby, I suddenly was not so sure. Why did I have to look at Lenin anyhow? I knew his face better than my own.

Lenin stared at us from everywhere. From postcards and paintings, from banners and pins, from teapots, from money. His statue was in every square. His head and shoulders in every hallway. As for his name, streets, parks, and sports arenas were named after him. Even the city we lived in was called Leningrad.

I shuffled by the mummy with my head turned away, but at the last moment, I could not help myself. I peeked. Lenin's face, glossy like fruit made of wax, glowed in the rosy spotlight. Just below his thin red beard, I saw a narrow strip of tape covered with paint the color of the mummy's skin, but this close, still perfectly visible. Oh, why did I look! Lenin had a bandage under his beard.

2

I STUMBLED OUT of the mausoleum, hanging on to my mother's arm. Why did Lenin have a bandage? Could a mummy scratch itself? I wondered if I could ask Dad about it, but no, it definitely would not be patriotic to ask him such a question.

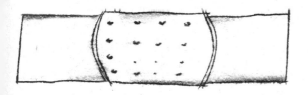

The Red Square was only white now. It was snowing. Behind the snowflakes, the American colors were flashing toward their bus. The Americans would be gone in a minute.

A picture of Lenin's bandage caked over with rosy paint appeared in my mind. The color made me ill. Why did we have to stay in line all day to see someone dead? Why did we have to learn a poem at school with the line "Lenin is more alive than all the living"? And why could these Americans take one quick peek at Lenin and board their bus to go back home and never have to see the mummy and its bandage again? Why?

I could not ask anyone, but a crazy idea shot through my head. If we ran fast now, my family could get on that bus to America, too.

Instead of us running, a young American— turquoise at the bottom, canary yellow at the top—sprung toward us. His colors sparkled so brightly in the falling snow that he seemed to float, and I wondered if our Soviet force of gravity did not apply to the Americans. He was yelling at us in his language.

"What is he saying?" Mom demanded of Dad. To the American, she said, *"Parlez-vous français?"*

Dad's face turned banner red. "Verboten, understand? Go away."

"Juicy fruit! Juicy fruit!"

The American thrust something into my brother's hand.

"Give it back at once, Victor!" Dad said.

"Say thank you, Victor," Mom said.

I was staring at the narrow strip of glossy wrapper in my brother's hand, the same shape as Lenin's bandage but of the brightest yellow. I could not take my eyes off it, but somehow, I also saw men running at us from all directions

and knew without being told that they were secret policemen disguised as regular citizens.

The American saw them, too. He turned around and bolted toward the bus. All at once, it got dark. A circle of men in black overcoats had closed around us.

"What did he give you?" one said to Victor.

The yellow wrapper disappeared into my brother's pocket.

"Leave my son alone!" Mom shouted.

"Excuse me?" the man said to Mom.

"No, young man! You will not be excused! Permitting foreigners to cut in line to see our beloved Lenin!

Outrageous! Your superiors will hear from me, you can be certain of that! Step aside, citizens. My son is expected at a national figure-skating competition."

"Figure skating, my ass," the secret policeman said. "Get out of here before I lock you up, you filthy yids."

"What are yids?" I asked my brother as Dad hurried us away.

"That's what some people call Jews," Victor said. "We're Jews—don't you know anything?"

I did not care. Being called a filthy yid did not matter to me at that moment. What mattered was the stick of American chewing gum in my brother's pocket. No chewing gum was sold in our country, and for a good reason. We barely had stuff to eat, let alone stuff to chew that you could not swallow.

For three weeks afterward, Victor chewed on that stick of Juicy Fruit. Nights, he soaked the chewing gum in a cup of tea to keep it soft. By the time I inherited the gum, it had neither taste nor smell. Still, it was better than what I used to chew while pretending to be an American—black chunks of tar left over from street paving. The tar was so hard, I broke a tooth on it once.

3

RUSSIA WAS CALLED THE USSR at that time, or the Union of Soviet Socialist Republics. If you think the name was long, take a look at an old Soviet map. One sixth of the world was painted red just to make the name fit.

Those old maps were made to trick our enemies. In case a foreign army invaded us, it would get lost. Lakes and forests on the map were drawn incorrectly on purpose. Rivers flowed in the wrong directions. Mountains were missing.

The Soviet borders ran for so many miles that when the sun rose at one end, it was already setting at the other. No matter how vast our borders were, they were so perfectly guarded that nobody could sneak in. Nobody could sneak out, either.

My brother told me that leaving the USSR for a trip to a foreign country was forbidden unless you were an important government official or had a terrific talent for something.

"I bet you didn't even know we live behind the Iron Curtain," Victor said to me once.

I pictured a huge curtain made of iron hanging along our borders.

"Sure I did," I said. "What's the iron curtain?"

"Not what you think," he said.

Victor told me that the Iron Curtain was not a curtain at all but a bunch of friendly countries along our western borders. To keep our neighbors friendly, Soviet army tanks, loaded with ammunition and ready for action, were stationed right

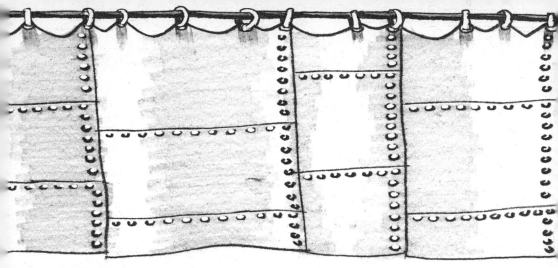

inside their countries. Our tanks scared everybody, not only our friends, but also those who lived across the ocean, our enemies.

"It's the Americans," Victor said. "It's their fault we live behind the Iron Curtain."

"Why?" I said.

"We're at war with them now. Only it's not a real war.

It's mostly talk. That's why they call it a Cold War. But in my opinion, it's not even that cold. It's lukewarm."

"Why do they call it cold, then?"

"Because it's not hot, don't you get it? The Americans and us built so many nuclear bombs, we could blow up each other in seconds. That would be a Hot War, then. Would you want that?"

Victor told me that instead of fighting a hot war, our government was carrying out strategic strikes by sending the most talented athletes and dancers to foreign countries to prove to the Americans that we are better than them.

"I'm going for sure," he said.

"Going where?"

"To foreign countries. I have a talent for sports. I'll be a figure-skating champion."

I knew that he would. He had won that competition in Moscow.

BECAUSE LENINGRAD is not that far from the Arctic Circle, our winters were perfect for sore throats, nasty colds, and pneumonia. Before I was allowed outside in the winter, Mom swaddled me in layers of itchy wool. Thermal underwear, padded pants, felt boots, sweaters, scarves, mittens—I could hardly move. When Mom tied the flaps of the fur hat under my chin, I could not hear either. Deaf, bulky, and nearly blind, I was told to go outside and play with the other children.

"Look, it's Yelchin!" one of the Russian boys having fun in the snow would yell, and pitch a snowball in my direction. I was an easy target, but my itchy armor protected me from their attacks.

After my brother explained to me about the war with the Americans, I began to think of our courtyard as the Cold War battlefield. My mother's swaddling was my personal Iron Curtain that kept me safe from the enemy.

THE BEST THING about the Cold War was that Americans had plenty of their own talent with which to strike back at us. Their mightiest weapons were movie stars and rock stars.

Once a week, my brother would take me to the tiny movie theater inside the Kirov's Palace of Culture to watch American movies. The movies were old and scratchy because they used to belong to the Germans until we beat them in World War II, or the Great Patriotic War, as we called it. That was why every movie began with a shaky card that looked like this:

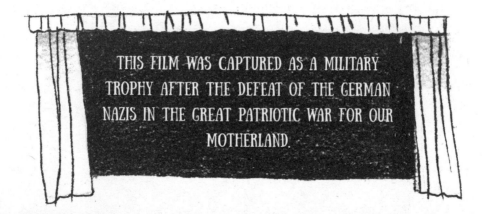

THIS FILM WAS CAPTURED AS A MILITARY TROPHY AFTER THE DEFEAT OF THE GERMAN NAZIS IN THE GREAT PATRIOTIC WAR FOR OUR MOTHERLAND.

The German translations of what the American actors said in the movies popped up at the bottom of the screen. The translations were useless. Victor and I did not know German, but amazingly the Americans in the movies spoke Russian.

"They dubbed the Americans into Russian," Victor once whispered to me in the dark, "so they won't say something bad about our country."

I did not care. I was not interested in what the Americans had to say. I did not follow their stories. Tap dancing and slipping on banana peels seemed sort of silly. All I wanted to know was what that mysterious universe called the United States of America looked like. Even though that universe was in black-and-white like ours, it looked nothing like Russia.

6

EVEN BETTER THAN MOVIES was American rock and roll. But you could not hear it on the radio, and you could not buy American records in stores. The first time I heard rock and roll, it was on a record some Russian fellow made in his apartment. My brother brought the record home, but it did not even look like a record. It was an old X-ray photograph of someone's broken leg with a pea-size hole burned at the center. A bunch of concentric

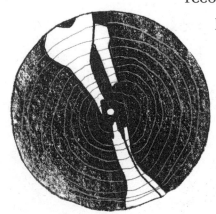

grooves spread out from that hole, like rings in a puddle after you toss in a rock.

My brother slapped the X-ray on the turntable, and when the broken leg began to spin, he dropped the needle and cranked up the volume. I had never heard anything like it. I could not tell a single musical instrument besides a drum and I could not understand a word of what the singer was yelling, but it was better than the Red Army Chorus on the radio, better than my mother's ballet music records.

It was a riot.
I loved it.

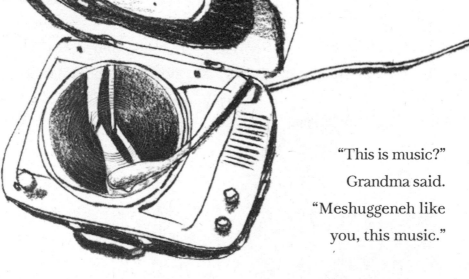

"This is music?"
Grandma said.
"Meshuggeneh like
you, this music."

"What's meshuggeneh, Grandma?" Victor shouted.

"Crazy. What else could such noise be? Crazy. Let me hear it again."

Grandma, Victor, and I listened to that X-ray for hours. We did not know the name of the song or who sung it, but we could not get enough of it. The code name for such records was *bones* because they were illegally recorded on X-ray pictures. They were in huge demand in Leningrad, but our government already had a special law against them called Groveling Before the West. Making and selling bones was illegal, and if we were caught, Victor said, we could all go to prison.

Maybe that was why when my dad came home from work, he said, "The Communist Party of the Soviet Union continues to defeat the tireless propaganda efforts of the United States of America" and threw the bones into our wood-burning stove. Grandma, Victor, and I put up a riot worse than any rock-and-roll band, forcing Dad to pull the X-ray out of the fire. The X-ray was so warped from the heat, we could not play it on the turntable anymore, but it played inside my head for weeks.

7

WITH ALL THE space to spread out in our enormous country, Mom, Dad, Grandma, Victor, and I were allowed to live in one tiny room. There were other rooms in our apartment, but other families occupied those rooms. The kitchen, the hallway, and the bathroom were considered communal spaces and we shared them with other tenants. Living quarters like ours were called communal apartments, or communalkas for short.

Each communalka had its own spy. Most of them were paid to spy, but some spied for free to be useful to our country. Our spy was Blinov. He lived by himself in the room next to us and spied on, eavesdropped, and reported on other tenants to the Committee for State Security, called the KGB for short.

The KGB wanted to know if any of our citizens were unhappy, and if they were, what was the reason. It must have been hard for Blinov to find out because our tenants never complained when he was around. They never even said *KGB* in their regular voices but in whispers as if it was a terrible secret.

Not once did I see Blinov leave the apartment. He sat in the corner of the kitchen, hidden behind the hallway door. You only knew that he was there by the tobacco smoke puffing up to the ceiling and by the tip of his slipper swinging in and out from behind the edge of the door.

My brother said that not everyone had to share communalkas with spies. Our important government officials and most talented citizens were allowed private apartments. Even though my parents did not know any important government officials, my mother had plenty of talented citizens for best friends.

8

Mom worked at the

Vaganova Ballet Academy, where children were taught to become great ballet dancers. The academy was named after the famous ballerina Agrippina Vaganova, but Mom—always in a hurry—called the academy the Vaganovka for short.

"The Vaganovka is the greatest classical ballet institution in the world," Mom would say with pride. "Mikhail Baryshnikov is a former student."

Mikhail Baryshnikov was the greatest Russian ballet dancer. He was allowed a private apartment, a personal car, and trips to foreign countries.

Baryshnikov danced for the Kirov Ballet Theater, which my mother also called the greatest classical ballet institution in the world. Citizens stood in line for hours to buy tickets to the Kirov but often by the time they reached the box office window, all tickets were sold. Fortunately there were always shifty characters loitering behind the box office that had extra tickets to sell to see Baryshnikov dance. Those tickets cost ten times the regular price of admission.

My mom's job at the Vaganovka was to make sure that her students cast in the Kirov's ballets knew their parts, were costumed, made up, and entered and exited the stage as instructed. Because of her job, Mom never had to stay in line to see Baryshnikov dance. The Kirov's special entrance for dancers, ballerinas, and orchestra musicians was always wide open to her. Mom was so well known in the world of classical ballet, I was convinced that she used to be a famous ballerina.

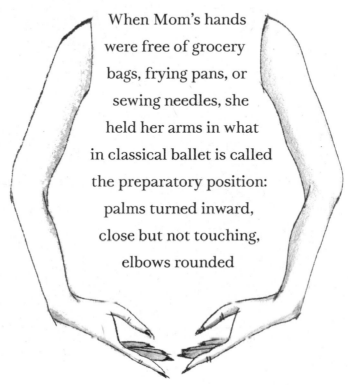

When Mom's hands were free of grocery bags, frying pans, or sewing needles, she held her arms in what in classical ballet is called the preparatory position: palms turned inward, close but not touching, elbows rounded

so there is plenty of room in between the arm and the armpit.

But it was not just her arms. Mom turned her feet out in a straight line called the first fundamental position of the feet. She walked in that position

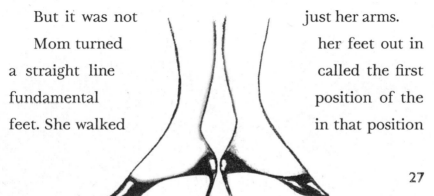

with such incredible speed that I had to jog to keep beside her.

I have often wondered if Mom kept herself in preparatory position in case a chance turned up to dance a pas de deux with Baryshnikov. A pas de deux is two dancers dancing together. Like everything in classical ballet, it's in French. Mom knew all the words. When she thought that I might have to go to the toilet, she would ask me in French. That would not be half as embarrassing had Mom's voice not been so terrifically loud. You could hear her ask me if I need to *pipi* or *caca* from two blocks away.

9

THE FIRST TIME my mother took me to see

Baryshnikov dance, I must have been ten or eleven. A grown-up man hopping around in tights was the last thing I wanted to see. But when Mom put on her prettiest green velvet dress, I changed my mind. She would only wear that dress on special occasions, and I thought we would sit in front-row seats. I was wrong. With Mom, ballet was strictly backstage.

As always, Mom was in a hurry. We flew in through the Kirov's special entrance,

up the steps, past the fireman in a brassy helmet asleep under the FORBIDDEN sign, and into total darkness, where the invisible orchestra was tuning their incredibly loud instruments. Mom kept her feet in the first position and zipped right through the dark, where mysterious things whooshed up and down and wheeled around us.

Everyone we passed was in a terrible hurry like Mom—the curtain was about to go up—but they all took time to tell her that she looked fabulous in forest green.

Proud to be with a fabulous-looking mother, I wanted to say that Mom made the dress herself out of an old ballet curtain painted to look like a forest, but I was not sure if she wanted her talented friends to know that.

"We'll be watching Baryshnikov from the wings!" Mom shouted over the blaring orchestra and whisked me into a narrow path between two dusty drapes.

The curtain flew up.

A flock of ballerinas tiptoed onto the dazzling stage. They smiled at us and said, "How do you do?" as they passed where Mom and I were standing.

The ballerinas left a cloud of powder in their wake. I

watched how prettily the powder swirled in the light beam and missed the ballerinas' dance. The audience clapped. The ballerinas rushed back, drenched in mud-colored sweat that ran down their faces, necks, and shoulders.

"Isn't it marvelous?" Mom shouted.

I was not so sure. The wings were dark as a cave and hot as an oven. The drapes were so full of dust that I was choking. And why were there no chairs? For ballet you need strong legs, but for watching ballet from the wings, you need legs of iron.

A terrifically loud bang from the orchestra punched me so hard in the belly that I doubled over and would have missed Baryshnikov's entrance had Mom not screamed, "Misha!" into my ear.

Russia's greatest ballet dancer leaped from behind a fluff of ballerinas and, smiling, soared incredibly high in the air inside the cone-shaped light.

"Grand jeté from fifth position!" shouted Mom.

I waited for Baryshnikov to land, but the spotlight seemed to hold him afloat on the swirling dust motes.

I looked at my mom. Her hands were clasped under her chin as if she was praying. Her eyes sparkled with tears. "Oh, Misha," she gushed at Baryshnikov, and, looking at me, added, "I wish *you* were born with such artistic talent, Yevgeny!"

The audience leaped from their seats, shouting "Bravo!" and flinging bouquets at smiling Baryshnikov.

10

"HAVE I EVER TOLD YOU about the first time I saw Misha?" Mom said to me on the way home from the Kirov.

She had, about a million times, but I did not want to interrupt her because she was already telling me again.

"He came from Riga to audition for us at the Vaganovka. Thousands of hopefuls audition each year, but only a handful is accepted. Make no mistake, Yevgeny, it is the fiercest of competitions."

She stopped, looked me up and down, sighed, and went on.

"That memorable day, we were in the exam room, all quite exhausted having tested boys and girls since the morning, when . . . in walks Misha."

Mom lifted her chin and walked ahead of me, pretending to be young Baryshnikov entering the room.

"His general appearance was striking. Noble carriage. Capable legs. Expressive and dignified manner. In a word, Misha was astonishing."

Mom smiled at her memory, looked back at me, and her smile went away.

"Don't slouch, Yevgeny," she said. "Stand up straight."

WHEN WE GOT HOME, Dad was already moving the furniture. Our room was so small that every night Dad had to move all the furniture out of the way in order to unfold our beds. He swapped things around as if he was shuffling jigsaw pieces to puzzle together a picture. I loved pictures, but I hated puzzles. The puzzle pieces were made in a particular shape on purpose so they could fit in one way only. But what if you did not like the picture they formed and wanted to change it? You were not allowed.

No matter how much Dad shuffled the furniture, Grandma's dining table took up most of our room. The table was as large and as old as Russia. Dad wanted to replace Grandma's table with a smaller one, but Mom would not allow it. Grandma was old, but she was younger than the table. Mom said that having that table kept Grandma going on account of not being the oldest in the room.

Victor usually helped Dad solve the furniture puzzle, but when he was late from his figure-skating drills, I would help Dad instead.

I volunteered to help with the furniture out of guilt. I knew I was a disappointment to my father. Dad had expected me to

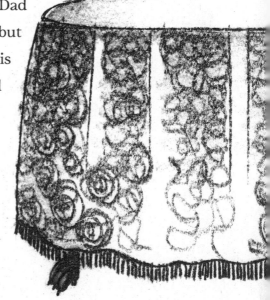

follow in my brother's foot-
steps and be a great athlete.
He tried me in every sport,
chess included, but I failed
in each. Dad had never
complained, but I could see it
there in him.

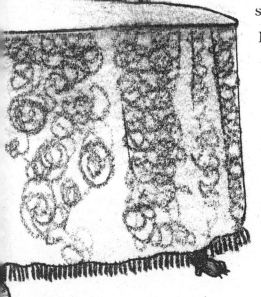

Dad was a little strange, two
people at once. Most of the time he
was a tight-lipped communist with
the Cold War on his mind, but when it came to Russian
poetry, Dad was a different person. One wall of our
tiny room was lined with shelves
stacked with poetry books.
Dad read those books so many
times, he knew each rhyme
by heart. Ask him to recite a
poem and Dad was pure fire!
He put so much feeling into
the rhymes—shouting and
whispering and flailing his
arms—that watching him was
beautiful and weird.

The night after I saw Baryshnikov dance, Dad and I were shuffling the furniture around and I asked him to recite a poem. Instantly he burst into rhymes. I waited for a moment while he was gathering breath and said to him, "You may not be aware, Dad, but Mom is in love with Baryshnikov."

He thought that was funny.

"I tell you, Mom loves him more than—"

I was about to say *more than you*, but I did not want to hurt Dad's feelings, so I said, "She loves him more than me."

"Don't be ridiculous, Yevgeny. Mother loves you very much."

"Why did she say 'Oh, Misha!' then, and start crying? We were at the Kirov watching Baryshnikov dance from the wings. You know what that is? The wings? And Mom said, 'I wish *you* were born with such artistic talent, Yevgeny!'"

"So what?"

"So does it mean I don't have any?"

"Any what?"

"Artistic talent?"

Dad's face was, as people say, an open book. He looked embarrassed. Even his hair, or what was left of it, stuck out in all directions, as if each hair was trying to run away from my question.

"You don't have to answer, Dad."

"No, no, no . . . I'm pleased that you're interested in artistic talent, Yevgeny, since your, uh, athletic talent is . . . Well. We won't go into that."

He shook off his slippers and climbed onto Grandma's table. During the day, our sheets, blankets, and pillows were piled high up on top of the wardrobe. He reached up to grab a pillow when Mom's voice thundered from the kitchen. Dad froze, listening.

Apparently one of the tenants had cut in the line to the

only toilet, and Mom was using foul language to express what she thought of such rude behavior.

"Hope it's not Blinov she's yelling at," Dad said.

"Forget about Blinov, Dad! Let's talk about Baryshnikov!"

Dad handed me the pillow and reached for the blanket.

"Your mother admires Baryshnikov for his artistic talent, Yevgeny, and she said what she said because . . . well . . . because having talent is important in our country."

"Why?"

He stared at me from above as if he was weighing something—something heavy—and was not sure I was old enough to hear the answer.

"Talent makes you *free*, Yevgeny," he finally said.

"Free?" I said. "Free to do what?"

"To live a better life. To have the privacy of your own apartment. To own a car. To travel to foreign countries."

He handed me the blanket.

"But, Dad! What about those Americans we saw in Moscow? Remember? One gave Victor chewing gum? They traveled to a foreign country, ours."

"So what?"

"What do you mean, so what? If Americans are free to travel, does it mean they all have talent?"

Right before my eyes, Dad transformed himself from a passionate lover of poetry to a tight-lipped communist.

"This conversation is over, Yevgeny. You're not old enough to discuss such matters."

The door flew open and banged against the edge of the table, shaking it so hard that Dad lost his balance. I thought he would crash to the floor, but he managed to catch the cast-iron loop that held our ceiling fixture. He looked funny, hanging there like a fish off a hook, but I knew not to laugh.

Grandma squeezed in sideways.

"With all her French, my daughter has some mouth on her. You will not hear a mouth like that on me."

She looked at Dad dangling from the ceiling.

"What's this? A circus? Your wife is yelling at that shtick dreck Blinov. You want to bring up children by yourself with circus tricks? Go fetch her."

She smiled at me. "The street talk your mother is talking, I didn't teach her such talk. I want you to know, Yevgeny."

"I know, Grandma. What's a shtick dreck?"

"A shtick dreck?" Grandma shrugged. "Let's say it's a poopy head in our language."

12

ONCE OUR BEDS were fitted together, the only space left for me to sleep was under Grandma's table. I slept on a cot, a narrow strip of canvas fastened to a folding frame with metal springs. The springs stretched the canvas in all directions and turned my cot into a trampoline. If I wasn't careful, the cot would bounce me to the floor. By the age of five, I learned to sleep without moving.

Every night I would climb under the covers, Dad would lift the tablecloth, slide my cot under the table, say "Sweet dreams," and let the tablecloth fall behind me like a curtain at the end of a ballet.

The tablecloth hanging to the floor on all sides turned the space under the table into a snug little tent. The glow from our stove flickered on the underside of the table, and the syrupy smell of pine from which the table was made tickled my nostrils. My little tent was as private as private could be, and yet I was not alone. My family was right there beside me. Dad said that if I had artistic talent, I could have a private apartment. But what did I need a private apartment for if I could sleep under Grandma's table?

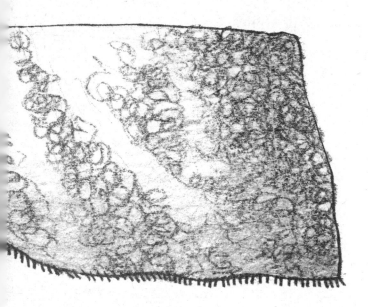

13

AT LIGHTS-OUT, Dad's voice came from the direction of the bed that Mom and he shared: "All right, people, who took my pencil?"

"He wants his pencil again?" Grandma said from her loveseat. "What is it with his pencil night after night?"

Victor, whose bed was made up of three chairs roped

together side by side to help him practice figure-skating balance while
he slept, said, "What do you
need your pencil
for, Dad?"

"I have a
thought, if you
must know. I
need to write it
down."

"Tomorrow you
write it down," Grandma
said.

"What if I
forget it by
tomorrow?"

"Wasn't much
of a thought, then,"
Mom said. "Lights out,
citizens."

The light clicked off, but
it was not the time for me to sleep yet. I waited until my
family settled into their dreams, then I snuck a stubby

pencil from under my pillow. I stole that pencil from Dad every night to draw on the underside of the table. The pine boards above me were covered with my drawings like a ceiling of a prehistoric cave. I had plenty of room to draw on. The table was big. My drawings were small. You know how small because the pictures in this book are the ones I drew on the table. I do not mean that these are the exact same pictures. I am drawing them from memory.

When you own as little as my family did, drawing on furniture is definitely a bad idea. I would have gotten in terrible trouble if my Dad had found out, but I could not help it. Life seemed like an enormous puzzle to me then, and drawing helped order the pieces: Mom, Dad, Victor, Grandma, Lenin, the Americans, even Baryshnikov. Each piece was a different shape. I was a puzzle piece, too, but I was made in such a wrong shape that I was convinced I would never fit in anywhere. The only place I fit in well was under Grandma's table, drawing to the soft squeak of the stolen pencil.

14

I WAS ON MY THIRD drawing that night when Mom and Dad started whispering under the covers.

"I took Yevgeny to see Misha tonight."

"I know. He told me."

"Did he tell you how marvelous Misha was? His grand jeté from fifth position was spectacular."

"He said you love Baryshnikov more than him."

There was a long silence.

Then Mom whispered, "As if loving your children was enough in this country. How will he survive without talent?"

"I tried to explain it to him, but he's still so young."

"Being young has nothing to do with it. Victor was a regional champion at his age."

"Victor's super. No problem with Victor."

They were quiet for a while, probably thinking how super Victor was. Then Dad whispered, "I'm really worried about Yevgeny."

"You're the only one worried?" Mom whispered. "I'm worried, too, for your information."

"We can't expect miracles. So the boy has no talent. At least he is healthy."

"Healthy, I don't know. He's too skinny."

"He eats well. Finishes everything on his plate."

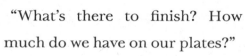

"What's there to finish? How much do we have on our plates?"

Dad didn't say anything, probably feeling it was his fault that we did not have much on our plates.

"Without talent, he'll never have a decent life . . . like some people," Mom whispered.

"Like Baryshnikov, you mean?"

"Yes, like Baryshnikov! Why do you think I dragged him to see Misha dance?"

"You're talking crazy, woman! Yevgeny our next Baryshnikov? He can't play a game of chess without knocking over half the pieces."

"Who's talking chess? He has an artistic streak . . . hidden somewhere. I can feel it. Maybe Vaganovka could bring it out of him."

I waited for them to go on whispering, but they were silent. Then Mom began to snore. The mattress creaked. Dad must have turned to face the wall. Next, he was snoring, too.

I had always tried to make my pictures on Grandma's table look like the world as it appeared to me, but after listening to my parents whispering that night, I drew a picture of the world as I wanted it to be.

I drew Mom crying in the wings and looking in awe at someone tour jetéing from fifth position. Only that someone was not Baryshnikov.

15

"WHAT DOES DRAWING CORRECTLY teach us, children?" asked Zinaida Ivanovna one day at the start of art class. "Drawing correctly teaches us to live by the rules. Discover the joy of living in our beloved country."

I raised my hand.

"What is it, Yelchin?"

"Can drawing help us discover if we have artistic talent?"

"You don't have to worry about talent, Yelchin. Be quiet."

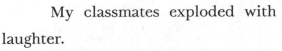

My classmates exploded with laughter.

Zinaida Ivanovna smiled and went on, "The right way to learn drawing, children, is by drawing from nature."

"Like trees?" I said.

"Are you trying to be funny, Yelchin? Even being a class clown requires talent. I'm sorry, but I don't hear anybody laughing."

Which was not true. My classmates were laughing.

"To draw from nature, children, means drawing objects taken from real life. Like this beautiful cube, for example."

When my classmates saw a plaster cube on Zinaida Ivanovna's desk, they stopped laughing. The cube was dust-colored, chipped on one side, and depressing. What kind of nature that cube came from I did not know, but I had to draw it like everyone else.

Zinaida Ivanovna walked up and down the aisles, making helpful comments about what was not allowed. Pressing on our pencils too hard, turning our papers upside down, holding our erasers while drawing, because our sweaty hands made the erasers dirty.

I finished drawing my cube and looked around. Everyone was still working. Their pictures looked about the same. Instead of drawing from nature, they were copying Zinaida Ivanovna's cube that she had chalked on the blackboard. She had used the ruler to draw the edges. Everyone in class used theirs, too.

My cube looked a little wobbly because I drew it freehand. I also placed it at the bottom of the page instead of

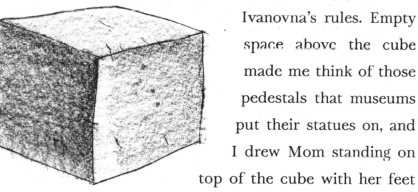

at the center, as per Zinaida Ivanovna's rules. Empty space above the cube made me think of those pedestals that museums put their statues on, and I drew Mom standing on top of the cube with her feet turned out in first position.

Vadik Berdyouk, who sat behind me, yanked the drawing from under my pencil and passed it around. My mother standing on the cube struck my classmates as funny. Then Zinaida Ivanovna got hold of my drawing.

"Very nice, Yelchin. You simply excel at never following the rules. Who is that standing on the cube?"

"My mom."

My classmates fell off their seats now, shrieking *my mom*, and choking from laughter.

"Yelchin was asking about artistic talent, children, remember?" She held up my drawing for everyone to see. "Judging by this disgusting caricature Yelchin drew of his poor mother, we can say with absolute certainty, children, that he has no talent whatsoever."

And as she crumpled my mother into a paper ball, the school bell began to ring.

16

VICTOR HAD ALWAYS been
the world's greatest athlete in
training. He excelled in every
sport—soccer, arm wrestling, chess—
you name it, but the reason he
became a champion in figure
skating was because my dad
caught him risking his life on a
pair of bootless skates.

As soon as the streets turned icy, Victor used to hide
in the archway of our apartment building, ready for action.
Skates were secured to the soles of his shoes with wire,
and an iron hook—the kind butchers use to hang meat—was
concealed under his coat. The moment an occasional truck

rumbled by, Victor would dart out, slam the butcher's hook over the truck's wooden tailboard, and skate behind its rear at neck-breaking speed.

I was convinced that sooner or later my brother would kill himself, but I kept my promise not to tell Mom and Dad about his suicidal rides.

One day, I was watching Victor from under the archway—I was not yet allowed to go out in the street by myself. I saw Victor dash after the passing garbage truck, and in the same instant noticed Dad crossing the street. The garbage truck cut him off, and Dad turned to yell at the driver—and caught sight of my brother hooked to the truck's tailboard.

Dad stood with his mouth open, watching his oldest whisked around the corner by the skidding truck.

I knew it was against the rules, but I could not help breaking them at such an important moment. I ran out into the street.

"Are you all right, Dad?"

It took him a moment to answer. "What are *you* doing in the street?"

"I've never done it before, Dad. I'm sorry."

"And what about your brother? How long has this been going on?"

"He's never done it before, either, Dad. I'm sure he's sorry, too."

Just then a different truck rumbled by, pulling Victor in the opposite direction.

Dad's head snapped to follow my brother leaping over the tracks of the streetcar like a rabbit ducking bullets. When Dad turned back to me, he was smiling.

"We'll try the hooligan in figure skating," he said. "He should do fine."

FIGURE SKATING WAS ONE

of our government's best weapons in the Cold War battles. No expense was spared on grooming talent, and when ready, our most talented young skaters were sent to international competitions to beat the Americans. In return, our champions were rewarded with private apartments, personal cars, and trips to foreign countries.

In no time, my brother become an ace figure skater. Dad and I went to his competitions and even to some of his practice sessions. Mom, who did not care for sports, accepted figure skating because it was a kind of ice ballet set to music.

Soon, Victor's coach decided that my brother was too good to skate by himself. From single skating, he was switched to pair skating. He was paired up with a girl named Irina. To twirl Irina over his head, Victor needed big

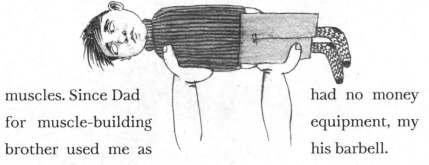

muscles. Since Dad had no money for muscle-building equipment, my brother used me as his barbell.

I was too light to be a barbell, but I was good at keeping still, straight, and quiet. Victor lifted me over his head and pumped me up and down in series of twenty. I was happy to be Victor's barbell. During those weight-lifting mornings, my brother and I had our best conversations.

A couple of weeks after I eavesdropped on my parents whispering at night, Victor was pumping me up and down from a standing position.

"Remember that one time when we saw Lenin's mummy in Moscow?" I said.

"Yeah."

"Lenin had a bandage under his beard, did you know that? How could a mummy cut itself?"

"Shaving."

"Shaving? Isn't he dead?"

"He didn't shave himself, stupid. They had special people doing it."

I did not want to think about someone shaving a mummy, so I changed the subject.

"Zinaida Ivanovna said I have no talent."

"Zinaida Ivanovna is a moron. What does she know? And it's not your fault, anyhow."

"What's not my fault?"

"That you have no talent."

When Victor lifted me up again, my nose scraped ceiling plaster and a speck fell into my eye.

"What's wrong, kid?" he said, dropping me down to his chest.

"Nothing."

"Nothing? You have tears in your eyes."

"It's not tears. A piece of plaster got into my eye."

Victor lowered me onto the edge of Grandma's table and gently flicked the plaster from my eye.

"It's easy for you," I said. "Mom and Dad think you're super, but try to be me for a day. I can't fit in anywhere without talent. Even in our family!"

"What are you talking about?"

"They don't love me."

"Who?"

"Mom and Dad."

"Don't be stupid. Of course they love you."

"No. I'm bad at sports, so Dad is always disappointed, and Mom loves Baryshnikov more. She took me to the Kirov to see him dance and . . ." I told him what she said.

"Know why she took you there?"

I did not.

"Use your brains, kid. Mom wants you to be good at something. What you do is you say, 'Thanks for taking me to see Baryshnikov, Mom. I'm crazy about ballet now.'"

I loved my brother. He always knew how to give me hope.

"You think I can be a dancer?"

He laughed and slapped me on the back.

"Of course not. But you tell her you want to be like Baryshnikov, and she'll love you to death—I guarantee it."

I NEVER TOLD

my mother that I wanted to be like Baryshnikov because I did not want to be like him. Plus, I couldn't. Nobody could. To draw pictures under the table was all I wanted, but even that was getting harder to do. Growing up must have been so tiring that I would be dead asleep before I could even begin drawing.

I was in high school when the opportunity finally came up to follow Victor's advice. I wish I didn't. It nearly ruined my life.

I know it happened on a Friday, because Friday was our turn to wash the floors. Once a week, each family took a turn at washing the floors of the communal spaces in our apartment: the kitchen, the hallway, and the bathroom, which was just a closet with a toilet in it. The schedule had been agreed on years before I was born. All families did their share, but the floors remained perfectly filthy.

When I came home from school, Mom and Dad were on their knees scrubbing the floors with rags soaked in soapy water. Mom scrubbed the kitchen floor. Dad scrubbed the floor in the bathroom.

I climbed onto the windowsill to tear old newspapers into the little squares we used for toilet paper.

"Why don't you read to us from those squares, Yevgeny?" Dad said from the bathroom. "Educate your parents on the achievements of our Motherland."

"'Poverty and unemployment in the United States of

America had increased by 36.5 percent,'" I read from the first square I tore from the newspaper, "'while our standard of living continues to rise.'"

Mom dipped her rag into the pail of filthy water. "They call this *living*?"

"'Every twenty-one seconds,'" I read from another square, "'a crime such as murder, kidnapping, or theft takes place in the United States.'"

"At least they have something to steal," Mom said. "What do we have?"

Dad's head popped out from the bathroom.

"Very nice." He made big eyes in my direction. "In front of the boy."

"'The stars of the Soviet ballet,'" I read from another square, "'are preparing a program of beloved Russian classics for a tour abroad. The first stop of the tour is scheduled for Toronto, Canada.'"

"They don't even mention Misha's name?"

"No, Mom. Is he going?"

"Yes, he's going!"

She smacked her rag into the pail, fished it out, and throttled the dirty water out.

"The stars of the Soviet ballet? Who are they kidding? A bunch of talentless has-beens allowed abroad because they're bootlickers and snitches! Misha is the only real talent among them, and they don't even mention his name!"

Dad's head popped out from the bathroom again. "I'm warning you, woman. Please watch your mouth."

"What did I say?"

"I heard what you said."

"I didn't say it. I whispered it."

"*Your* whisper they hear in America. They hear it in the Big House, too. They hear it loud and clear."

Dad ducked back into the bathroom.

"What's the Big House, Mom?" I whispered.

"It's the KGB, darling," she whispered back. "The Committee for State Security? Blinov works there. Because of creeps like him, Misha's tremendous talent is wasted."

"What does Baryshnikov have to complain about?" Dad hollered from the bathroom. "I'm cleaning toilets, and he's dancing at the Kirov!"

Mom was rubbing the grease off the floor so hard that I could tell she was very upset.

"They don't mention Baryshnikov in the paper," Dad kept hollering, "because they're worried he might stay behind. My opinion? Your Baryshnikov is thinking of defecting."

"Stop it!" Mom covered her ears. "I can't bear the thought of losing Misha!"

Every now and then, our great talents did not come back from trips to foreign countries. Not coming back was called defecting. A gross word that sounded like *defecating*, which means taking a poop. Each time I overheard that someone had defected, I had imagined one of our talents stuck in the airport bathroom taking a poop and missing the plane back home.

Dad was in the bathroom and Mom was on her knees facing away from the hallway, but from where I sat on the windowsill, I suddenly noticed tobacco smoke puffing up to the ceiling and the tip of Blinov's slipper swinging in and out from behind the hall-way door.

Blinov, the KGB informer, had been in the kitchen this whole time!

"Mom?" I whispered, and nodded at Blinov's slipper.

"Mark my words," Dad hollered from the bathroom. "Baryshnikov is not coming back. Those foreigners are waiting for him with open arms."

"Shut your mouth!" Mom shouted when she saw Blinov's slipper.

"Now she says shut your mouth! Did *I* call Blinov a creep or did *you* call Blinov a creep?"

In the same instant that Dad poked his head out of the bathroom, Blinov stepped out from behind the hallway door.

"So handy at scrubbing the floors, the Yelchins are."

The cigarette stuck to his lower lip bopped up and down as he spoke.

"I heard of a place not as nice as this that needs its floors scrubbed. I suggest you keep that in mind, comrade-citizens."

Dad's mouth shaped the letter O, and through that O a

tiny sound escaped, a pitiful whimper. He ducked back into the bathroom and locked the door behind him.

Blinov grinned and winked at me. Leaving dirty smudges across the floor that Mom had just washed, he shuffled up to the bathroom and knocked.

"Give us a holler when you're through, Comrade Yelchin. I need to take a dump."

19

AFTER BLINOV WENT to his room, the bathroom door creaked open and Dad stepped out. Mom was still on her knees. They did not look at each other, and they did not say anything. Never had I seen my parents so scared.

I was scared myself. What if Blinov sent us all to prison? Something had to be done, but what? The only way to cheer up Mom was to say something nice about Baryshnikov. Suddenly I was struck by Victor's advice that I had almost forgotten. I was not sure if telling Mom at that particular moment that I wanted to be like Baryshnikov was the best idea, but I had no time to think up anything better.

"Watch this, Mom!"

Giving myself a good running start, I stuck my arms out like wings and leaped at her. It felt great while I was up in the air, but  landing, I slipped on the wet floor, slid into the pail, and splashed Mom head to toe with dirty water.

"Yevgeny!" Dad shouted. "The heck are you doing?"

Mom began crying.

"Stop yelling at the child," she whimpered, lifting her soaked dress away from her body.

"Then you yell at him!"

"It was an accident. Right, darling? An accident."

"It was no accident! He leaped!" Dad shouted. "Didn't you see him leap?"

I snatched the newspaper off the windowsill and tried to dry Mom's dress with it.

"Yes, Dad, I leaped! I did! Ever since Mom took me to the Kirov . . . I've been . . . I've been practicing ballet!"

My ears were burning from lying.

"I want to study at Vaganovka, Mom! I want to be like Baryshnikov!"

I was told to wait in the hallway while my parents had a serious discussion in our room. I did not have to wait long.

Within two and a half minutes, I was informed of the official decision.

The auditions for the Vaganova Ballet Academy were not until the summer, but Mom would present me to the artistic director Konstantin Mikhailovich in the spring.

20

IT WAS A LONG TIME until spring. I was hoping that they might forget about presenting me to Konstantin Mikhailovich, but almost every night Mom kept mentioning my audition before she turned the lights off. She was very excited.

I had disappointed my father with my lack of athletic ability. Now it was my mother's turn to be disappointed with my dancing. I could not bring myself to ask her what I was supposed to do to make myself presentable to Konstantin Mikhailovich, so I decided to strike ballet poses in front of our mirror instead.

That mirror must have been used in a fun house until some- one had the bright idea to stick it on the door of our wardrobe. My reflection ballooned, shrank, and wiggled, but what choice did I have? I learned from Mom's ballet book—the only book that she owned—that ballet dancers must practice before the mirror.

The author of the book was Agrippina Vaganova, the very same Vaganova after whom the greatest classical ballet institution was named. The title of the book was as strict as the instructions on its pages—*Basic Principles of Classical Ballet: Russian Ballet Technique.*

For weeks, I could not get past the first section, "five

Fundamental Positions of the Feet." I tripped over myself and bumped my head against the mirror from the first.

While I tortured myself in front of the mirror, Grandma listened to the radio. Lately the radio kept blaming Russian Jews for some war or other that was going on far away in Israel.

"It is well known that during the Great Patriotic War," the radio said, "the great Russian nation saved the Jews of the Soviet Union from complete extermination."

"They're talking extermination already?" Grandma said. "They move fast."

"And how do the Jews pay back the Russian people for their selfless struggle?" the radio said. "By deception, treachery, treason."

"Oy vey, they're talking treason now," Grandma said. "Turn that thing off, Yevgeny."

"I can't, Grandma," I said. "I'm in attitude."

I was trying to balance on one leg in attitude, which Vaganova described as "a pose on one leg with the other lifted at an angle of 90 degrees and carried back, bent at the knee."

"You hurt your leg, Yevgeny?"

"No, Grandma. It's nothing."

"He stands on one leg for nothing. You a stork?"

"I'm practicing ballet."

"With a bad leg?"

She stared at me for a moment.

"You look upset, darling. You're worried about the radio?"

"No, it's not the radio, Grandma."

"Then come tell your grandma what's wrong."

I set my leg down and collapsed next to her on the loveseat.

"Mom said that Konstantin Mikhailovich of the Vaganovka would evaluate me on five things."

"Only five? What, he's that busy?"

"One: my general appearance; two: my body proportions; three: my musicality; four: my coordination; and
five: the level of my artistic talent."

"If it was ten, you would pass!"

"How, Grandma? Mom and Dad think I have no
talent."

"They're talking extermination and treason on the radio
and your meshuggeneh parents worry about talent?" she
said. "In my day we worried about our children, talent or no
talent. Love was enough."

"That was a long time ago, Grandma. I heard Mom say
that loving children is not enough anymore. She said I
would not survive without talent."

"Talent you have enough for two, Yevgeny. What you
need is a little freedom to show it, but they make you sleep
under the table."

"I like sleeping under your table, Grandma. It's
quiet."

"You call it quiet? For years I couldn't get any sleep with
that squeaking."

"What squeaking?"

"Do I know? Squeak, squeak, squeak. We had a mouse
maybe."

Grandma must have heard Dad's stolen pencil squeaking on the underside of the table.

"I heard it, too, Grandma," I said, ashamed to be lying to her. "We had a mouse maybe."

"Greetings, sports fans!"

My brother burst into the room, darted to the wardrobe mirror, and grinned at his reflection. His head was bandaged. Dry blood caked the dirty gauze.

"Already they're beating Jews?" Grandma said.

Victor rolled up his shirtsleeves and flexed his muscles. His forearms bulged in the fun-house mirror.

"Nobody's beating anybody, Grandma. It's from a hand-to-hand lift. Irina slashed my forehead with her skate."

"Mazel tov," Grandma said. "Good news at last."

She heaved herself out of the loveseat and shuffled out of the room.

Next, we heard her scream in the kitchen.

21

OUR NEIGHBORS STOOD in small packs, looking at Grandma. She sat on the floor at the threshold of our apartment before the front door, which was flung open. I thought she had slipped and broken her leg, but when I came closer, I saw what had made her fall. Someone had drawn a Nazi swastika on the door and written below it: *Beat yids–save Mother Russia!*

"Dimka did it!" Victor shouted,
and bolted past Grandma and
down the steps into the courtyard.

I tried to lift Grandma off the
floor, but she was as loose as jelly. I
could not lift her. I looked to our neighbors for help, but
no one moved. They just stood there staring at me while

the kitchen radio went on talking about the Russian Jews helping the American and Israeli intelligence services to destroy our Motherland.

"Why don't you go to Israel, Grandmother?" our neighbor Nikulin said. "We don't want you here."

I dragged Grandma toward the hallway. Her woolen skirt bunched up over her thighs, showing two slack elastic bands clasping Grandma's stockings to her lilac underpants. Because our neighbors could see my grandma's underpants and because the radio kept saying that the Jews were bad, I felt so ashamed that I began crying.

"Move aside, young Yelchin."

Blinov nudged me away and lifted Grandma to her feet.

"For shame, little mother. Such scenes at your age . . . I ought to report you."

The tenants parted as Blinov half walked, half dragged Grandma toward our room.

"Don't cry, boy." Our neighbor Ermakova held out a cookie to me. "Have a cookie. You yids like sweets."

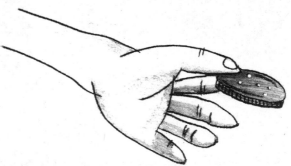

22

IN THE COURTYARD, my brother was beating Dimka Kryoukin. A dozen kids stood at a safe distance, watching. The dirty gauze unspooled from Victor's head, showing a deep gash across his forehead.

He was bleeding and Dimka was bleeding and you could not tell whose blood was whose.

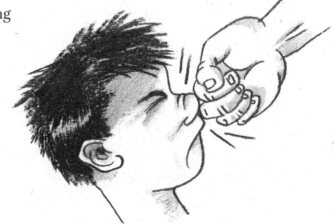

I had never told my brother that every time Dimka Kryoukin caught me in the courtyard, he hit me in the face. Dimka liked to say that if yids did not leave for Israel, they would all die horrible deaths. He had described those deaths to me, too. He was the lowest scum in our courtyard, but watching my brother beat him, I could not help feeling sorry for Dimka.

That was when Dimka's grandmother came down into the courtyard. I thought she would rush in to stop my brother, but she just stood there, watching, her eyes squinted into machine-gun slits.

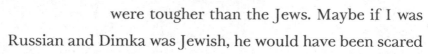

"Put up a fight, you sissy," she told Dimka. "Show the yid who's in charge."

I was amazed. My grandma lost it at the sight of a swastika on the door, but this Russian woman not only kept her cool watching her grandson getting bloodied but egged him on to keep fighting. I wondered if the Russians were tougher than the Jews. Maybe if I was Russian and Dimka was Jewish, he would have been scared

of me instead of me being scared of him. That would have been good for both of us, because I would never draw a swastika on his door or punch him in the face.

Finally Dad came home from work and hauled my brother away.

"Apologies, Comrade Kryoukina. I'll have a serious talk with Victor—don't you worry. This is unacceptable behavior."

I wondered if Dad would still think it was unacceptable behavior when he saw our front door, but when we walked up to our apartment, the swastika and the ugly words were gone.

The next day, my classmates knocked the air out of me at recess. They said things like: "You gonna cry, yid?" and "It was just a joke!"

It probably was a joke, because the boys who beat me also happened to be my best friends.

At home, the radio kept blaming Jews for things even Victor could not explain to me. Grandma refused to leave the room and had to use a potty instead of standing in line for the toilet with our neighbors. Every night, Mom and Dad whispered under the covers about what they heard on the radio or what they saw in the streets. I was so scared that I had stopped sleeping well and went back to drawing, but my pictures under Grandma's table became a little shaky. Soon we would all die horrible deaths, just as Dimka Kryoukin had always promised. But nothing happened. We did not die. Everything went back to how it was before except for one terrific thing: after my brother bloodied Dimka's nose, Dimka kept away from me for good.

23

SPRING CAME AT LAST and with it, my dreaded audition. The day before I was to be presented to Konstantin Mikhailovich of the Vaganovka, Mom ordered Dad to take me to the public bathhouse for a thorough washing.

You would always hear everywhere that personal hygiene was a matter of political importance to Soviet citizens, but it was not easy to stay clean. One cold-water sink was all we had in our communalka.

Every day, Dad and Victor rubbed under their armpits and behind their necks with cold water. I only washed my hands and brushed my teeth, which was plenty of washing for me, but once a week I had to go with Dad to the public bathhouse. It was a long walk. Good thing Dad knew every building in the city where the great Russian poets had died.

"See that café across the street?" Dad pointed to a yellow building on the corner of Nevsky Avenue. "Literary Café, opened in 1816. The great Russian poet Mikhail Lermontov used to dine there. And in 1837, the even greater Russian poet Alexander Pushkin met his second there on the way to a pistol duel."

"Did he win, Dad?"

"You should know that, Yevgeny. Pushkin was mortally wounded and died, at age thirty-seven. A tragic loss for Russian poetry."

"What about the other guy?"

"Lermontov? He was killed in a pistol duel, too—in 1841, at age twenty-six."

They should have put time aside to practice target shooting in between rhymes, but I did not want Dad to think that I was disrespectful to his favorite poets, so I said, "Poets don't live very long, do they, Dad?"

He stopped and looked at me for

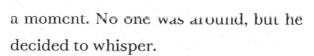

a moment. No one was around, but he decided to whisper.

"You can never be a great poet, Yevgeny, if you're afraid to tell the truth. But truth is a dangerous thing. Most people don't like it. Did I ever tell you what our great poet Osip Mandelstam once said?"

"I don't remember, Dad. I'm sorry."

"'Poetry is so respected in Russia,' Mandelstam said, 'that poets are killed for it.'"

Dad glanced over his shoulder, then looked back at me, concerned.

"Forget what I just told you," he whispered. "I was just kidding."

24

To get a proper wash in the public bathhouse, you needed three things: a bench to sit on, a washbasin, and a bar of soap. The soap we had.

Dad found an empty bench, told me to stay put, and went off in search of the washbasins. I had been in that bathhouse a million times before, but each time it felt weird to be without clothes in front of strangers. I sat on the edge of the bench, looking away from the naked men glistening behind the clouds of steam.

Across from me, a man sitting on a bench was so thickly covered in soapsuds that he looked like a snowdrift. Two veiny hands broke through the snowdrift, raised a wash-basin, and dumped the steaming water over itself. The soapsuds rushed to the floor, and when the top half of the man came into view I saw a face with a heroic mustache tattooed across his chest. The man saw me looking at his tattoo.

"Know who that is?"

I shook my head no.

"They don't even teach him at school no more?"

He struck the tattooed face with his fist.

"Comrade Stalin, our great leader and teacher, a man of great talent."

I was instantly interested.

"What kind of talent?"

"You name it, brother, Comrade Stalin had it. Great genius of humanity he was. For thirty years, he held our country in here."

He raised his clenched fist to show me. I guessed that

was where the man with a mustache held our country, in his fist.

"Everyone 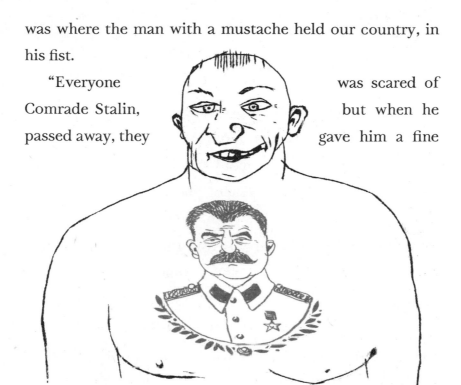 was scared of Comrade Stalin, but when he passed away, they gave him a fine

funeral, stuffed him according to science, and put him next to Lenin in the mausoleum."

"I didn't see him there."

"That's what I'm trying to tell you, brother. They took him out! The man who built this country from nothing. Who beat the Germans. Who would have beaten the Americans, too, if not for the yids. The yid doctors poisoned him. Did you know that?"

He tilted his head and studied me for a moment.

"You wouldn't be a yid yourself now, would you, brother?"

I thought of Dimka's grandmother, who kept her cool while Victor thrashed her grandson, and I thought of the bad things the radio said about the Jews. I thought of my best friends kicking me at school, and I lied to the man.

"No," I said.

"No, what?" Dad emerged from the steam, washbasins under each arm. "What are you telling my son?" he asked the tattooed man.

"We were just having a friendly chat, comrade," the man said. "Nothing to worry about."

He looked from my dad to me then back to my dad. His nasty smirk told me he knew we were Jewish.

"A nice little boy you have here. Honest little boy."

25

ON THE WAY HOME from the bathhouse, Dad and I always stopped at the beer hall. Not a hall exactly—a low-ceilinged cellar, smelly, smoky, swarming with drunks. There were no chairs. We stood behind a tall narrow table that was crawling with flies and sticky with spilled beer. We got a mug of foamy beer for Dad and a dried salty fish for me. The fish looked like some prehistoric thing in the natural history museum, but it was delicious.

"Did we poison Stalin, Dad?" I said, nibbling on the prehistoric fish.

"Who are we?"

"The Jews. Is that why nobody likes us?"

"Who said nobody likes us?"

"The radio did."

"I don't think you fully understand, Yevgeny, what they say on the radio."

"What about the swastika on our door? Beat yids—save Mother Russia? What's so hard to understand about that?"

Dad sat the beer mug down and wiped the foam off his chin.

"I heard what that man in the bathhouse told you. He was a liar, Yevgeny.

Nobody poisoned Stalin. He died because he was old."

"How old?"

"Seventy-five."

"The guy said that Stalin built our country from noth- 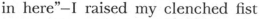 ing, and beat the Germans, and for thirty years held our country in here"—I raised my clenched fist to show him where Stalin held our country—"and he lived to seventy-five? How come poets die so young, Dad? Is it harder to write poems than scare people?"

"Lower your voice. You don't want people to hear."

"Why not?"

"We don't talk about Stalin anymore, Yevgeny. He was our leader, that's true, and he did accomplish important things, but he also made some . . . some mistakes."

"So what? I make mistakes at school, Dad, and the teachers always scold me for them in front of everybody. What kind of mistakes did Stalin make?"

"Mistakes, Yevgeny. Leave it at that. He was criticized for his mistakes at the Communist Party Congress and—"

"Was he there?"

"Who?"

"Stalin. Was he there when they criticized him for his mistakes?"

"No, no. He was dead by then."

"Then it doesn't count, Dad."

26

THE NEXT DAY, there were many surprises. The first surprise was that Mom kept me home. She decided that extra sleep before I was presented to Konstantin Mikhailovich was more important than going to school.

While I slept, she had laundered and ironed my shirt, underwear, and socks and made my old school uniform look as if it was just bought from the store. I was to wear Victor's leather shoes that she had given such polish I could see myself better in them than in our fun-house mirror. Next, she rubbed some smelly stuff into my hair and slicked the comb through it until my head was a shiny helmet.

"Put your glasses on," Mom said to Grandma. "How does he look?"

"I need glasses? The boy looks gorgeous."

"Are you sure?"

"What is it? An eye test? I see perfect. Twenty-twenty both eyes— ask my doctor. Come here, sweetheart."

"DON'T TOUCH HIM!" Mom shrieked. "You'll mess up his hair!"

"I can see myself in his hair," Grandma said, hugging me. "Go get them, Baryshnikov."

We lived pretty far from Vaganovka, but Mom, worried that I would get wrinkled in a crowded streetcar, chose to walk.

Halfway there, lightning flashed, the skies cracked open, and rain poured. Mom snatched my hand and we took off at a run, leaping over streams, ducking under awnings, and sloshing through the flooded sidewalks.

It was fun until we finally reached the greatest classical ballet institution in the world.

We rushed through the freezing Vaganovka's lobby, tore up the steps to the second floor, and at full gallop burst into the clean, white high-ceilinged hallway.

Behind each door, pianos played different tunes, dance shoes knocked and scraped the floors, and stern voices shouted—

"Bend it! Bend it more!"

"Throw the leg, Grigory!"

"Eyes! Clear eyes! Give me your eyes!"

What were they doing in there? Were they torturing kids? If Konstantin Mikhailovich took me in, would they

torture me, too? Would they force me to throw my legs to the teachers and give them my eyes?

I was about to admit to Mom that I had lied to her about wanting to be like Baryshnikov, but she stopped so abruptly that I bumped hard into her.

"Remember, Yevgeny," she whispered into my ear, "Konstantin Mikhailovich is a genius, an extraordinary dancer in his time. It's a great privilege to be presented to him, so . . . so no need to be nervous."

She wiped the raindrops off my face and fixed my collar. Her hands were shaking.

"Walk in, take a bow, and stand quietly. You're very good at this, sweetheart. Listen carefully to what Konstantin Mikhailovich tells you and follow his instructions exactly."

She stared at me for a moment.

"I want to tell you something important, Yevgeny. Dad and I don't expect miracles. No matter what happens in there, we'll always love you. You know that, sweetheart, don't you?"

She gave me a quick hug, took a deep breath, and knocked on the enormous double door beside us.

27

"ENTERRRRRRR!" someone called out in the fake voice that actors use in theater plays.

I could tell that Konstantin Mikhailovich, a genius and an extraordinary dancer in his time, had been waiting for us because he had taken the time to arrange himself in an elegant pose. His right arm was gracefully placed on top of the enormous grand piano, his left bent at the elbow and folded into the pocket of the expensive-looking coat, and the toe of one brilliantly polished shoe reached the heel of the other brilliantly polished shoe in (I suddenly remembered!) the fifth fundamental position of the feet.

He nodded to Mom's apologies for being late, remarked about the inconvenience of rain, and said without looking at me, "Take your clothes off."

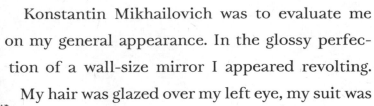

Konstantin Mikhailovich was to evaluate me on my general appearance. In the glossy perfection of a wall-size mirror I appeared revolting. My hair was glazed over my left eye, my suit was soaked, and I had lost one of Victor's shoes.

"Is he hard of hearing?" said Konstantin Mikhailovich.

"What?" Mom said.

"I suppose it runs in the family. IS HE HARD OF HEARING?"

"No, no, Konstantin Mikhailovich."

Blushing, Mom whispered to me, "Take your clothes off so Konstantin Mikhailovich can evaluate your physique, Yevgeny."

I struggled out of my mud-splattered clothes. Mom snatched them off the floor and held them to her breast.

"My son's name is Yevgeny, Konstantin Mikhailovich. His dream is to become a great ballet dancer like Baryshnikov."

Konstantin Mikhailovich made a sour face.

"I am dismayed Baryshnikov is trusted with a foreign tour. Personally I find him unreliable."

He glared at me shivering in my underwear. "Jump."

I looked up at Mom. Should I jump?

"All I hear about is Baryshnikov's talent," Konstantin Mikhailovich went on. "But whom does his talent serve, my dear madam? For whom exactly is he dancing? For our beloved people? For our beloved Communist Party? For our beloved Motherland? No, my dear. He does not! Baryshnikov is wasting his talent on himself, as if . . . as if he simply *likes* to dance! It is outrageous, in my opinion."

He glared at me again.

"Do you refuse to jump?"

"Yevgeny?" Mom whispered. "Don't keep Konstantin Mikhailovich waiting. Jump!"

I did not want to jump for Konstantin Mikhailovich, but the way Mom was looking at me, I knew I must jump for her. I must grand jeté like Baryshnikov and soar all the way to the ceiling. I must amaze this phony man with my artistic talent and make my mother happy.

And so I jumped.

Before my feet left the floor, they slapped down again. The grand piano replied to my landing with a long and tragic *dong*. Konstantin Mikhailovich smiled at himself in the mirror.

"My dear madam, I am perfectly aware that in your youth you aspired to become a ballerina, but cruel fate had decided otherwise."

What was he talking about? What cruel fate?

"And now, my dear madam, you are presenting your offspring to amend what was denied you in your youth. I applaud your . . . doggedness. The boy, however? How shall I put it? The boy lacks entirely in the required qualities of the danseur, such as pleasing general appearance, adequate body proportions, and coordination. Thus, my decision. Are you ready?"

Mom was afraid to look at him. She nodded at the puddle she had dripped onto the brilliantly polished floor.

"In gratitude to your service and devotion to the Vaganova Ballet Academy, I am willing to overlook the boy's complete lack of artistic talent. If he passes the medical examination, we will take him for a trial period of one year."

He glared at me.

"No need to thank me, boy."

So I did not.

28

MOM TELEPHONED Dad's office to tell him the exciting news.

"Yes! Yes! Yes!" she shouted into the phone. "Konstantin

Mikhailovich agreed to take him! What? No. It's not official yet. Yevgeny must pass the medical examination first. What? Worried? About the medical examination? Why should I be worried? He's a healthy and beautiful child. What? I never said he was skinny. He eats well. Finishes everything on his plate. What kind of question is this? Of course, he's happy. Wait. He'll tell you himself."

She pressed the phone against my ear.

"Daddy wants to know how happy you are. Tell him, darling."

"Dad?" I said into the phone. "The guy said that I lack entirely in the required qualities such as pleasing general appearance, adequate body proportions, and coordination, but he was willing to overlook my complete lack of artistic talent."

"Wonderful! Wonderful, Yevgeny!" Dad shouted. "Congratulations!"

To celebrate my success, Mom bought me a cup of vanilla ice cream. We sat on a park bench. The sun was shining, wet trees sparkled like diamonds, and pigeons splashed in the puddles.

It was nice.

"Can I ask you a question, Mom?"

"Of course, honey. Go ahead."

"Konstantin Mikhailovich said that in your youth you had aspired to become a ballerina, but cruel fate had decided otherwise. What does that mean?"

Mom shrugged and said, "Agrippina Vaganova didn't accept me to the Academy when I was your age, honey. She said I did have the required qualities, but . . ."

"But what?"

"It wasn't about me. She couldn't take me because of my father."

"Your father? You mean my grandfather? What did he do, Mom?"

She smiled, but it was not a happy smile.

"He didn't do anything wrong, Yevgeny. It was just a mistake. Please don't ask me again."

And when her smile was gone, her face became as hard as my dad's face in the beer hall.

I wondered if not letting Mom become a ballerina had something to do with that Stalin fellow. It must have been one of those mistakes Dad refused to tell me about.

"You know what's funny, Mom?" I said to cheer her up. "I'd always thought you were a famous ballerina."

"Did you?"

"Because of the way you look."

She laughed, pleased.

"But I'm glad you're not a famous ballerina, Mom. When I was a little kid, I was always afraid that you might defecate."

"Yevgeny! Defect, not defecate."

She suddenly looked worried, probably thinking about Baryshnikov going to Canada soon.

29

THAT NIGHT FROM under the table, I heard Dad complaining as usual: "I'm warning you, people, if my pencil is not returned immediately, I'm going to body-search everyone!"

"I'm ready," Grandma said.

Mom said, "Go to sleep."

"If I could sleep, would I be asking for my pencil?"

"Sure you ever had it, Dad?" my brother said.

"Sure I'm sure. What, are you calling me crazy?"

"Don't answer him, Victor!" Mom said. "Pretend everything is normal."

"If this is normal," Grandma said, "I'm Baryshnikov."

"Please, Mama! Leave Misha out of it."

Mom turned off the lights and began sighing.

"What's with the sighing?" Grandma said. "Someone died?"

"What I love about Misha," Mom said in the dark, "his magnificent talent, is the very thing that'll make me lose him. The Americans will take one look at his grand jeté and snatch him away."

"You can stop sighing," Dad said. "Your Misha will return. Think Blinov didn't report on me? They'll watch Baryshnikov like hawks on that tour. Like hawks they will. He'll have no chance of defecting."

"How do you know?"

"After what I said in the kitchen?"

"Will they listen to you?"

I could hear hope in Mom's voice, but when Dad did not answer, I knew that he was just trying to make Mom feel better.

30

WHEN MOM TOOK me to see Baryshnikov again, he was dancing Prince Albrecht in the ballet called *Giselle*, his last appearance before he left for Canada. The performance was sold out weeks in advance, and the ticketless citizens hoping to squeeze in for free swarmed all entrances.

The Kirov's lobby was buzzing like a beehive. Everyone was terribly excited, still Mom managed to inform every person we passed that Konstantin Mikhailovich had agreed to take me on at Vaganovka. Mom's friends were very happy for me. They shook my hand and slapped me on the back. By the time we reached the backstage door, the ballet had started. Mom tilted her head to one side and listened to the orchestra.

"Act one, scene one. The gamekeeper who's in love with Giselle is trying to convince her that Albrecht is a nobleman disguised as a peasant. Giselle ignores him."

The fireman in the brassy helmet was guarding the door.

"Not allowed."

"What do you mean not allowed?" Mom said.

"Step aside at once, Petr Ivanych."

"Can't do. The house is sold out. The wings are packed above the allowable capacity. What if we have a fire? What then? All exits are obstructed."

"Why should we have a fire? What nonsense!"

"Do not raise your voice at me, Comrade Yelchina."

120

"Who's raising whose voice?" Mom shouted. "STEP ASIDE, PETR IVANYCH!"

I tugged at her sleeve. "Let's go home, Mom."

She glared at me, offended by my ridiculous suggestion, grabbed my shoulders, and shoved me at the fireman.

"Look for yourself, Petr Ivanych! My son Yevgeny! Accepted, by the way, to the greatest classical ballet institution in the world! Whose graduates include the greatest dancer in ballet history, Mikhail Baryshnikov, by the way! Who at this very minute dances Prince Albrecht in the disguise of a peasant, while we're wasting time talking to you, you ignorant brute!"

At that moment, three men in black suits puffing on cigarettes passed under the

NO SMOKING! sign. The fireman leaped aside and stood at attention while the men filed in through the backstage door.

"Simply outrageous!" shouted Mom. "Why are you letting them in?"

Before the fireman could slam the door after the men, the last in line paused to look over at Mom.

"You should be ashamed of yourself, Yelena Yakovlevna, disrupting the performance with such behavior. Of all people, you should know better."

Guess who it was! Our neighbor Blinov, the KGB informer!

"I ought to thank you for my promotion, Yelena Yakovlevna. My report about the devious plans of defection by Comrade Baryshnikov was taken seriously. Not that my superiors didn't already suspect."

"Blin?" someone called out from the other side of the door. "Coming or what?"

"Coming, coming," Blinov called back, and turned back to Mom. "They're sending me on the tour, Yelena Yakovlevna. First time to a foreign country. I'll be by Comrade Baryshnikov's side at all times, so don't you worry your little head about him. He'll be back—I promise."

Blinov leaned toward me so that his eyes were just inches from mine. His eyes were cold and colorless like two splinters of ice.

"A little birdie told me you might be starting the ballet school in the fall? Congratulations, young Yelchin, that's a privilege. But did you know we don't allow children at the Vaganova Ballet Academy whose fathers and mothers are—"

"Leave my child alone!" Mom yanked me away from Blinov.

He leaned back, smirking, puffing on his cigarette.

"I suggest you raise your political awareness, Yelena Yakovlevna," he said, blowing smoke into my mother's face. "Ballet is not just silly dances, you know. Comrade Baryshnikov is our weapon in the struggle against the United States of America. In case you forgot, it's the Cold War, my dear."

31

A FEW WEEKS LATER, Blinov disappeared. All that was left of him was the stench of tobacco smoke behind the kitchen door. Nobody in our communalka knew what had happened, but tenants, relieved not to be spied on, talked louder in the kitchen and even complained about our government.

One morning, we saw the door to Blinov's room wide open and all of his stuff gone. Next, a nice young couple with a baby and a Siberian tomcat moved into Blinov's room. The cat's name was Misha, same as Baryshnikov's.

My mother and I never did get to see Baryshnikov dance before he went to Canada, but we could see his face every time we passed a display of the Leningrad's most talented youth set up about two blocks from our apartment building. A red banner ran below a bunch of black-and-white photographs:

LONG LIVE THE PARTICIPANTS OF THE
COMMUNIST YOUTH CONGRESS!

That congress had ended ages ago, but the photographs of the youths who had participated in it and the red banner were still up, soggy from spring showers. Every time Mom

passed the display, she would stop to admire the photograph of Baryshnikov, the first one on the left, and say a thing or two about his artistic talent. But after Baryshnikov left for Canada, Mom would hurry past his photograph without stopping, looking like she was about to cry. Baryshnikov, too, looked miserable in the picture. He was meant for flying through stage lights, not sitting through boring speeches at the Communist Youth Congress.

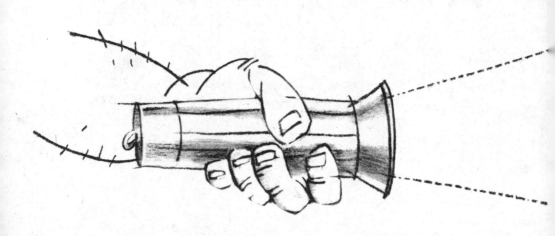

32

IMAGINING BARYSHNIKOV flying in the lights made me terrified about Vaganovka. Come fall, not only I but my mom, too, were up for one serious humiliation. If I could not fit anywhere other than under my grandma's table, how could I ever fit into the greatest classical ballet institution in the world?

In the end, it was my father who saved me. He had such a brilliant thought one night that he got out of bed in search of his pencil and found me drawing under the table.

"What's going on here, Yevgeny?"

He pointed the beam of his flashlight made in communist China at my hand holding the pencil.

"Please, Dad, don't be mad."

He snatched the pencil from me.

"My son is vandalizing furniture with my stolen pencil and I should be mad? It's wonderful! I couldn't be happier!"

"I'm sorry, Dad."

"Why should *you* be sorry? You're having a good time. It's me who's losing brilliant thoughts every night."

"I'm sorry, Dad."

"One more sorry out of you and I'm turning violent—I'm warning you."

Dad had never turned violent before. I was safe, but I felt bad about taking away his brilliant thoughts.

"Why can't you get another pencil, Dad? We're not that poor. And also . . . what kind of brilliant thoughts do you have?"

"Do I remember what kind of brilliant thoughts? That's the whole problem!"

He pointed the flashlight at the bottom of the table covered with my drawings. He stared at them for a long time.

"Good God," he finally said. "I had no idea."

Next, all the lights in our room were ablaze.

"Wake up, people!" Dad was hollering. "We got a genius under the table!"

33

THE VERY NEXT DAY, Mom came home with a present.

"I kept these at work because I wanted to give it to you on your first day at Vaganovka, but . . ." She handed me something wrapped in brown paper. "A little big, sweetheart, but don't worry—I'll take them in."

I squeezed the package, trying to guess what was inside.

"Open up already," Grandma said. "I may not live this long."

I tore the package open and nearly passed out.

"That a present?" Grandma said, disappointed. "A pair of britches?"

"Don't call them britches, Grandma! These are blue jeans made in America by Levi Strauss!"

"A Jew made those britches?" Grandma said. "Let me feel them."

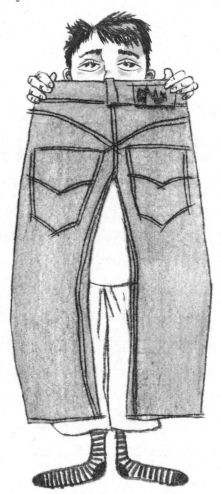

I had seen blue jeans in the old American movies my brother used to take me to, but I did not know then that the jeans were blue, because the movies were in black-and-white. But lately, American tourists had flooded our city, and most everyone, even the ladies, wore blue jeans.

I had really wanted a pair, but like any American goods, blue jeans were not sold in our stores. To approach foreigners was against the law, but wherever the Americans went, the same shifty characters that sold tickets behind the Kirov approached them. They bought stuff from the Americans and sold it at ten times what they paid to those Soviet citizens who wanted to look like they just returned from a trip to a foreign country.

"They must have cost a fortune!" I said. "What will Dad say?"

"Not a fortune. Misha gave me a very reasonable price."

"What?" I gasped. "These are Baryshnikov's jeans?"

"Yes, Yevgeny. These are Mikhail Baryshnikov's jeans."

Afraid to drop the jeans to the floor, I carefully set them on the table.

Mom smiled at me. "Perhaps you can't be our next Baryshnikov, Yevgeny, but at least you can have his jeans, and someday, I am sure of it, you'll fill them out as an artist in your own right."

"You're giving him used britches?" Grandma said.

"Very lightly used. Misha was selling his old clothes before he went to Canada."

"Why was he selling his old clothes, Mom?" I said. "Is he not coming back?"

Mom gasped and her hand flew to her open mouth.

34

USUALLY WHEN MY BROTHER burst in our room hurricane-style—loud, laughing, flexing his muscles—he made everyone happy. But this time, Victor did not burst in. This time, he snuck in, closed the door with such care as if it was made of glass, and stood sideways as if he could not look at Mom with both eyes.

"What's wrong?" she said, spinning the handle of her sewing machine.

I was leaning over Mom's shoulder, watching Baryshnikov's jeans getting shorter in the leg and tighter in the waist to fit me.

"You know those pictures down the street?" Victor said. "The Communist Youth Congress?"

I thought of Baryshnikov looking miserable in the soggy photograph. He must have been much happier now, dazzling foreigners in Canada with his artistic talent.

"The pictures are still up," Victor said quietly. "Except one."

Mom stopped stitching and looked up at Victor. "They took Misha down?"

Victor stared at his shoes.

"What does it mean, Mom?" I said. "Why did they take his picture down?"

Mom did not answer and went back to spinning the handle of the sewing machine. Her tears dotted Baryshnikov's jeans, which were getting smaller and smaller under the flickering needle.

ЕЗДА КОММУНИСТИЧЕСКОГО СОЮЗА МОЛОДЁЖИ!

35

BARYSHNIKOV DEFECTED, but not a word of his defection appeared anywhere. His name was never again mentioned on the radio, the television, or in the newspapers. The Kirov's announcements of its new season's ballets were printed with someone else's name assigned to dance Baryshnikov's parts. The greatest Russian ballet dancer vanished without a trace.

Thanks to Baryshnikov's defection, I never got to wear his blue jeans outside of our apartment. The first time I put them on, Mom's eyes swelled with tears. She left the room quickly, and by the time she was back, the jeans were folded and put away in the wardrobe. She did not mention it, but I could tell she was grateful.

The following day, I waited until Mom left for Vaganovka, put on Baryshnikov's jeans, and stood before the mirror, pretending to be an American.

"Give her poison better," Grandma said.

"What?"

"You want to kill your mama, better to give her poison than wear the britches."

Eventually, Grandma and I made an agreement. I could wear Baryshnikov's jeans in our room while Mom was at work. I could even wear them to the bathroom if no neighbors were in the kitchen, but by the time Mom was expected to return, the jeans had to be stored in the wardrobe.

A few months later, I was too big for the jeans. I was growing fast. Mom found out, probably from Grandma, that the jeans did not fit me anymore and suggested that I give them away. The very next day, some kid showing great promise at Vaganovka was wearing Baryshnikov's jeans.

36

A YEAR OR SO had to pass before I owned my own pair of blue jeans. They were almost new–I inherited them from my brother. Victor and his partner, Irina, became so good at figure skating that they were allowed to travel to foreign countries with our Olympic team. They didn't win any important competitions, but they brought back suitcases full of foreign outfits.

And I was in one of those outfits–very lightly used by my brother–when I came home one day to find Mom and Dad having tea with some strange lady.

She was about as old as Grandma, but if Grandma's face was all sharp angles, the lady's face was made up of circles.

"Allow me to introduce my son," Mom said. "Yevgeny, say hello to Tatiana Georgievna Bruni, our legendary ballet designer and most extraordinary artist."

"Your parents are telling me you have quite a talent," the lady said with a pleasant smile. "May I see your drawings?"

"She wants to see his drawings?" Grandma said. "She gets down on her knees to see his drawings."

"Mama!" Mom gasped, blushing.

"Hope her knees are strong at her age—that's all I'm saying."

"I can flip the table," Dad suggested.

"She wants to see his drawings," Grandma said, "she crawls like I crawled."

"I'm sorry, but . . ." The

lady looked around in alarm. "I don't understand."

"What is it? Rocket science?" Grandma said. "The boy draws underneath the table." She glared at my dad. "What are you sitting there for, Mr. I-Can-Flip-It? So flip it already."

While Dad was taking off his jacket and rolling up his sleeves, Mom cleared the table. The lady held her teacup in the air because Mom snatched away her saucer. The lady tried to set the teacup down without the saucer, but Mom yanked the tablecloth off the table. Startled, the lady scraped her chair back, bumped into the wardrobe, and spilled tea in her lap.

"Pardon me, Tatiana Georgievna," Dad said, and clutched the edge of the table. His face turned red, then purple, then blue. The table would not budge.

"A very old table," Grandma said to the lady. "They made things good in your youth. Solid oak."

It was not oak, of course. Plain old pine. But it must have taken three whole pine trees to build Grandma's table.

"I were you, I'd be calling a doctor," Grandma said to Mom. "Your husband is getting himself a nice hernia."

Mom and Dad exchanged panicked looks.

"I am sorry to have troubled you, Tatiana Georgievna," Mom said. "I don't know what I was thinking. Yevgeny's drawings are on the underside of the table and my husband can't seem to . . ."

But Tatiana Georgievna turned out to be a good sport. She laughed, got down on her knees, and crawled

under the table. Then my dad did, and then my mom, and then Grandma gave me one of her looks.

"What are you standing? He's standing! Get down there. That old lady is no small potatoes."

I crawled under the table. It was pretty crowded in there. I was not sure how to feel with all of them inside my private space, looking at my drawings.

"Your line is very nice," Tatiana Georgievna said. "Expressive."

Dad cleared his throat and said, "Your mother and I were talking, Yevgeny . . ."

"And since you decided . . ." Mom said.

"Since *we* decided," Dad said.

"Since we decided that Vaganovka was not a good idea . . ."

"We feel that . . ."

"So, lady? You like to show him the ropes?" Grandma shouted. "Or you just like to sit under my table?"

"Looks like you ran out of room here, Yevgeny," Tatiana Georgievna said, smiling. "Would you like to study art with me in my apartment?"

Instead of answering, I gave her a big smile. The biggest.

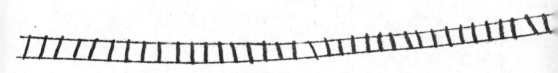

37

MOM INSISTED ON ESCORTING ME to my first lesson with Tatiana Georgievna. I tried to argue that I should go by myself, but who could argue with Mom?

We took a streetcar. The schoolbag in my lap held a brand-new sketchbook, pencils, brushes, and a box of watercolors. My art supplies cost Dad plenty, but as he had never mentioned it to me, I had made a secret pledge not to disappoint him this time.

"Do you know how fortunate you are to be taught by

"Tatiana Georgievna Bruni?" Mom said. "The Brunis are the most artistic family in Russia. Painters, musicians, architects. Two hundred years' worth of talent! Are you listening?"

I was and so were the rest of the passengers. Mom's voice thundered through the streetcar, describing artistic achievements of every Bruni in great detail. The passengers were listening to her with interest, getting a tour of our city's cultural heritage for the price of a streetcar's ticket.

"Tatiana Georgievna's great-grandfather Fidelio Bruni was of Italian descent. A remarkable painter. His greatest achievement is *The Brazen Serpent*, on view at the Russian Museum. Do you remember the painting, Yevgeny?"

Oh, yes, I remembered. Fidelio Bruni's greatest achievement was the largest painting I have ever seen, nearly twenty by thirty feet, and also the most horrifying. The painting was very popular with the museum visitors, either because it was so large or because Bruni chose to paint a story about God punishing Jews for complaining. To teach Jews a lesson, God dropped fiery snakes onto them from the skies. The snakes were so masterfully painted that they had given me nightmares.

As Mom kept talking and talking, those nightmares returned. I imagined that Tatiana Georgievna's apartment looked like her great-grandfather's enormous painting, and to teach *me* a lesson, she was dropping fiery snakes on my head.

At home, I had tried to convince Mom to let me go to Tatiana Georgievna by myself, but as we walked up the stairs to her apartment, I became so jittery that I asked her to come in with me. But no matter how much I begged her, Mom refused to be in the way of a meeting of "two artistic talents." She gave me a quick hug and dashed downstairs. I waited until the front door slammed down below, took a deep breath, and pressed the buzzer beside the brass plate engraved in cursive: *T. G. Bruni*.

Tatiana Georgievna opened the door.

"Come in, dear, come in. I was expecting you."

Her apartment was roomy and bright. No snakes anywhere.

Pretending that you just had a big meal when offered something to eat was a sign of good manners according to my mother, and that was why I firmly refused tea and chocolate éclairs. Tatiana Georgievna dismissed my refusal as nonsense and went to the kitchen to put on the kettle.

Clutching the schoolbag with the art supplies to my chest, I tiptoed around the room where I was to be *shown the ropes.* The walls were hung with the framed paintings, each signed *T. Bruni* in the lower right corner. The paintings were not as large as Fidelio Bruni's, yet they were no less weird.

I had been to every Leningrad museum by then, but I had never seen anything like this before. The people in those paintings must have been ballet dancers, but instead of tights and tutus, they wore costumes that looked like machines, work tools, and battleships. Their geometric shapes and eye-popping colors burst out of the frames and made me dizzy.

"What do you think of those, Yevgeny?"

Tatiana Georgievna walked in with a steaming teapot, cups, and a plate of plump chocolate éclairs on a tray.

"The pictures are for a ballet called *The Bolt.* Dima

Shostakovich composed the score. A crazy ballet with a crazy title, but we were all crazy then, young and naive. We believed everything was possible."

She sat the tray beside her easel.

"We were allowed one performance only. Somebody at the top ordered the critics to hate it and the ballet was closed. Luckily no one was arrested."

"Who was it? Who ordered the critics to hate it?"

"Try the éclairs, Yevgeny. They're delicious."

I looked at the pictures again. Arresting someone for putting on a ballet sounded like one of Stalin's mistakes. I wanted to ask Tatiana Georgievna to explain, but I didn't dare.

38

TATIANA GEORGIEVNA

had lots of wonderful books in her apartment. The books were about Russian artists, but they were printed in foreign languages. I had neither heard the artists' names nor seen their art in the local museums. The books had been given to Tatiana Georgievna as gifts from talented dancers, choreographers, and musicians who bought them while touring abroad.

I spent hours in her apartment painting copies of strange and  beautiful pictures I discovered in those books. I worked silently, not wanting to disturb Tatiana Georgievna at her easel, but each book I pulled off the shelf made her stop painting and look over my shoulder.

"Ah, Marc Chagall! What marvelous colors! magician. Born in Russia, A Jewish went to France, came back after the revolution to help our young country, but when the Communist Party took over the arts, Chagall left Russia again. Still in France, by the way. Still paints beautiful paintings."

I copied Chagall's goats, roosters, and green-faced Jews floating across cobalt skies as if our Soviet force of gravity had no chance to hold them down.

When I opened another book, Tatiana Georgievna said, "Kandinsky? Some claim that he invented abstract painting. Personally, I'm not convinced. I think Malevich did it. Malevich stayed in Russia and was banned from painting what he wanted, but Kandinsky went to Germany and kept making his gorgeous abstractions."

I copied Kandinsky and Malevich.

I had a huge stack of paintings by now, but they were so bad that even Chagall, Kandinsky, or Malevich would not have recognized their originals in my copies. Tatiana Georgievna did not seem to be bothered by my tilted and muddy pictures. She smiled, praised my efforts, and explained techniques for bringing my copies closer to what the artists had in mind.

At home, I was making my own pictures. They were nowhere near as good as anything I had found in Tatiana Georgievna's books, but I kept working, drawing and painting instead of doing homework. Soon I was way behind at school. I hid my terrible grades from Mom and Dad, but they did not seem to care to know. As long as I was practicing my artistic talent, my parents were perfectly content.

39

"I WONDER if there are two kinds of Russian artists," I said to Tatiana Georgievna after I went through all of her books. "Those who defect from Russia and those who stay home."

Tatiana Georgievna smiled at me from behind her easel.

"The defectors kept making the art they wanted to make," I said, "but those who stayed behind were not allowed to do that. Their art was banned. Some were arrested. Some were even shot to death."

Tatiana Georgievna kept painting, but she stopped smiling.

"But I think there's also the third kind," I said. "Those who neither defected nor were arrested or killed."

Tatiana Georgievna glanced at me. "Why were they spared, Yevgeny?"

"I don't know. Take, for example, my old art teacher Zinaida Ivanovna. It was in fifth or sixth grade, I think, she wanted us to draw a cube. She had one, very ugly, sitting on her desk. She drew the

cube herself on the blackboard first and then had everyone copy her picture instead of drawing the cube itself. You know what Zinaida Ivanovna used to call it? Drawing by the rules!"

Tatiana Georgievna laughed. "Did you draw by her rules, Yevgeny?"

"I wish I could. If I could follow her rules, I'd never get in trouble."

I thought about it for a minute.

"So those artists who stayed behind? Those who were spared? They were spared because they figured out how to make art by the rules. That's what I think."

Tatiana Georgievna continued painting in silence. Her brush barely touched the paper, leaving feathery strokes of soft and silky glow. Her painting was beautiful, but the only thing it had in common with the paintings for the banned ballet *The Bolt* framed on the walls was her signature in the lower right corner. Over forty years had passed since she had painted those pictures, but they were still vibrating under the glass as if they were alive. I could feel none of that vibration under Tatiana Georgievna's brush now.

I should have never said what I said about the artists who were spared by the government. The last thing I wanted was to make Tatiana Georgievna upset. It was not her fault that she was born a celebrated Bruni. If she had defected to some foreign country, she would have felt terribly guilty for breaking the two-hundred-year tradition of artistic talent in Russia. Had she stayed home and kept on painting her weird designs, she would have been arrested and possibly killed. Instead, Tatiana Georgievna chose to follow the rules. It was probably a good decision, but the price she had to pay for it was high. She had to settle for making pretty pictures instead of making great ones.

"I'll change the water for you, Tatiana Georgievna!"

I grabbed the water glass in which she rinsed her watercolor brushes and bolted for the kitchen before she saw me blush.

40

THEN THE winter
came and went and
then another winter
came. It was dark by four in the afternoon. By the time I
would return home from Tatiana Georgievna's apartment,
our street was pitch-black.

Once, someone jumped out at me from under our courtyard's archway. I spun around and started running, but the
man—it was a man—caught me by the shoulder and spun me
around.

"Dad! What the heck are you doing?"

"Did I scare you? Sorry, my dear, sorry. I was waiting for you."

He threw his arm over my shoulders, pulled me in tight, and began walking away from our house.

"Were you at Tatiana Georgievna's? Making great art together? I'm so proud of your talent, Yevgeny, so proud."

I could tell he was excited about something because he was walking incredibly fast. He sort of dragged me along at a trot.

"Where are we going, Dad?"

"Oh, just a walk, Yevgeny. Just a brief, vigorous walk. Good for your heart. In such excellent weather."

He drew a deep breath and exhaled a cloud of steam. It was about fifteen below.

"You'd be interested to know, Yevgeny, that our State Literary House has just released a book of poems by—"

"Dad? You have lots of books of poems already. What do you need—?"

"No, no, no, no! You don't understand, Yevgeny. A book of poems by Osip Mandelstam! The great, great, great Russian poet!"

Dad leaped up a little from excitement, slipped over an icy patch and fell, pulling me down with him. We sat in a snowdrift with our feet sticking out like stick figures I used to draw as a kid.

I looked at my dad laughing, and after a while I was laughing too. I was still laughing when he whispered into my ear, "But there's a catch, Yevgeny. We need a coupon. I'm counting on you."

Now I knew what that was all about.

Twice a year, Soviet schoolchildren were required to collect recyclable paper waste. Some big shot in Moscow assigned the amount of poundage school districts were supposed to collect. Come what may, each district had to deliver the pounds.

The collecting was organized as a "socialist competition" between the grades. We were split into teams and marched door-to-door to pester citizens for old newspapers, magazines, letters, packages, and anything else made of paper that could be recycled.

Schoolchildren didn't get anything in return for their labors, but if you were a grown-up and decided to join in, twenty-two pounds of collected paper would earn you a special coupon. You got that coupon stamped at the collecting stations where your paper waste was weighed. Like everything else in Russia, books, especially good books, were in short supply. As a reward for paper collecting, they let you exchange your stamped coupon for some great book you could never buy in a regular bookstore. Dad had gotten

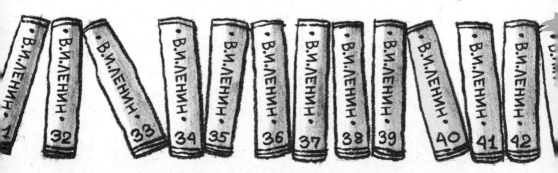

lots of his poetry books with coupons Victor and I earned for him.

"You think it's easy to round up twenty-two pounds of paper, Dad? You try it!"

Dad was too embarrassed to even look in my direction.

"Why can't you do it yourself, Dad? Other grown-ups do it. My friend Serega's dad, for example. He also wanted some book he could only get with a stamped coupon. He's a communist like you, Dad, a big cheese somewhere, a head of some factory or something. He's got no time for begging door to door. He asked Serega to help, but Serega said, 'Forget it, Dad—you want the book, you collect the paper yourself.' So guess what his father did? To save his valuable time? Guess, Dad, guess!"

He smiled, watching me laugh.

"What did he do, Yevgeny?"

"He went to the House of Books on Nevsky and he bought up three sets of complete works of Lenin. Lenin wrote a lot of stuff, Dad, did you know that? Fifty-seven volumes in each set. Multiply that by three . . ."

I looked at Dad for help.

"One hundred and seventy one."

"One hundred and seventy one books, Dad! Imagine how heavy they were! More pounds than he needed. Smart, right? But when he took the books to the exchange station to swap his Lenins for stamps, they called the KGB on him! Serega said his dad was in hot water for that one. They kicked him out of the Communist Party, took his fancy job away, and now he's a janitor or something. Isn't that funny, Dad?"

Had I not laughed so hard, I would have noticed that my father's kind, smiley face had become his tight-lipped communist face again. He scrambled out of the snowdrift, glared at me with disgust, and stormed away.

"Wait, Dad!" I shouted after him. "I'm sorry about Lenin. I'll get you that coupon—I promise."

41

DAD WAS too proud to mention the coupon again, but he could barely look at me. *Yes* or *no*—that was how far his conversations with me went. Once again I had disappointed my father.

He did not care that I still had to collect paper for school, attend classes, take lessons with Tatiana Georgievna, and make my own pictures. All he cared about was that fellow Mandelstam. If we had studied Mandelstam's poems in our

Russian literature class, I might have been more enthusiastic about Dad's request, but the only thing I knew about him was what Dad told me once on the way to the public bathhouse—that he had said, "Poetry is so respected in Russia that poets are killed for it."

Why would poets be killed if poetry were so respected? At first, it did not make any sense to me, but after studying Tatiana Georgievna's art books, I began to understand what Mandelstam might have been talking about. Poets were artists, too. If they did not make art by the rules, they were in trouble in our country. I did not know if Mandelstam was killed for his poetry, but asking Dad about it was useless. He would have never told me the truth anyhow. Still, I had to collect twenty-two pounds of paper. Whatever it took, I could not disappoint Dad again.

The idea to turn to crime came to me when I noticed that our schoolyard was overflowing with paper.

The waste was supposed to have been weighed and trucked off long ago, but for some important government reason, no trucks were available. We were told to continue with our socialist competition.

While we unloaded paper waste off our sleds, a loudspeaker in the schoolyard droned: "The USSR has climbed a mountain from where we can see our final goal— a thriving communist society." And a mountain it was.

Thousands of pounds of paper were slowly rotting in our schoolyard.

Daily after our classes ended, I joined my team on collecting expeditions, hauled what I gathered back to the schoolyard, and dumped my share at the foot of the mountain.

In the evenings, I returned to steal the paper.

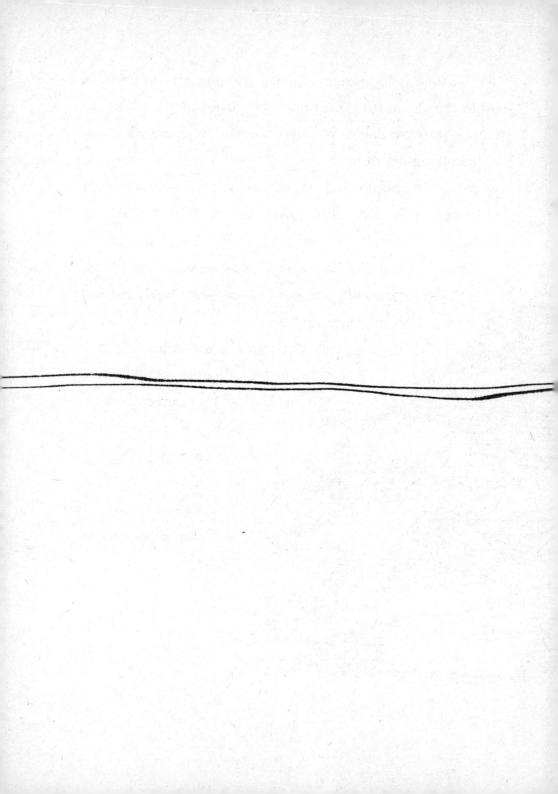

42

ONE NIGHT

when I came back
to the schoolyard, a girl I had never seen before sat atop the
mountain of waste. Wet chunks of snow fell from the skies,
hitting the rotting paper like snowballs, but she did not
seem to care. She was hunched over something that looked
like a book.

I piled my sled with stolen paper in a hurry. The
collection station was about to close, and the school's
custodian could still be prowling the grounds. I almost
left. Instead, I climbed the mountain to see what she
was reading.

"Get out of here," she greeted me.

"I thought you were reading a book, but it's just a photo album."

"Oh, please." She slammed the album shut. "A real genius."

"Genius under the table."

"What?"

"Nothing. It's stupid. That's what my dad called me once."

She squinted at me for a moment, then turned away and opened the album again. "Leave me alone, all right?"

I leaned over her shoulder to look at the photos. It was a family photo album, nothing unusual, black-and-white pictures glued to the black pages like in everyone else's album, except that someone's face had been snipped out with scissors from every picture.

"That's so weird!" I said. "My grandma's photo album is exactly like that. In the photos with my grandma and my mom, some other fellow is cut out. I don't even know who that fellow was."

The girl turned and looked up at me with interest. "Was your grandfather arrested?"

"Why would my grandfather be arrested?"

"There would be no other reason they cut him out, would there?"

Nobody had ever told me anything about my grandfather except after the ballet audition when Mom said that Vaganova could not accept her to the ballet academy because of her father.

"When the State Security arrested people," the girl said, "their relatives cut them out of their family pictures."

She opened and closed two fingers as if snipping someone out of a picture with scissors.

"Why?" I said.

"So they wouldn't be accused of any relationship to enemies of the people."

"What does that mean? Enemies of the people?"

"Could you not be such an idiot, please? That's what they called those who were arrested. Enemies of the people."

I had never heard of such a thing before. Was my grandfather an enemy of the people?

"My granddad was arrested in 1953," the girl said. "He was a doctor, but he was tried as an agent of international Zionism. They were arresting Jewish doctors then. My family never saw him again."

The man with the tattoo in the bathhouse had said

something about Jewish doctors. How they had poisoned Stalin.

"Was your grandfather Jewish?" I said.

"You're not listening. In 1953, they were arresting and shooting Jews. They were beaten in the streets all over the country. Stalin was going to round up all the Jews, put them in cattle cars, and send them off to Siberia to die . . . but he messed up, the butcher. He couldn't pull it off."

"Why not?"

"Uhh . . . Stalin died that year?"

She turned away from me and looked at the album again.

The wet snow kept falling, whacking the rotten mountain. I tried to imagine my family in a cattle car going to Siberia to die. Then I tried not to, but I could not get the picture out of my head.

"Why did Stalin want to do that? Send Jews to Siberia?"

The girl shrugged. "My mom thinks it was a provocation. The Americans would have gotten mad at us, and Stalin could have used it to start another war."

"Against the Americans? But that would be a nuclear war. Then we would all be . . ."

Someone was climbing up the mountain toward us.

"What the hell are you still doing here?" the man shouted.

I recognized Serega's father, the communist big cheese turned custodian for trying to swap Lenin's books for a stamped coupon. He snatched the photo album out of the girl's hands and flung it aside.

"Get out of here before I call the cops!"

43

WHEN I CAME HOME, Mom, Dad, and Grandma were watching the Leningrad Symphony Orchestra on our new TV, the first color set in our communalka. It came with an antenna that did not work, so Dad had to rig his own, a thick black wire snaking out of the back of the TV and climbing up the wall to hang from the ceiling like a spiderweb.

"Take your coat off, darling," Mom said, "and go wash your hands."

"Why should his hands be dirty?" Grandma said. "The boy is wearing mittens."

"What took you so long, Yevgeny?" Dad said.

He did not look at me, but I knew he was dying to know if I'd been out collecting paper for him.

Mom knew it, too. "In this weather, they make children gather papers," she said to Dad. "Should that be allowed, huh, communist?"

Dad began messing with the TV antenna.

To the drumroll from the symphony orchestra, I said, "Was my grandfather an enemy of the people?"

All three stared at me in astonishment.

"Was it you who cut him out of all the pictures in our album, Grandma? Or did you do it, Mom? Was it like a school project or something?"

"Oy vey," Grandma said, and clutched at her heart.

"What are you talking about?" Mom said.

"Did Stalin want to send all the Jews to Siberia? So he could start World War Three?"

"Yevgeny!" Dad shouted.

"Was that one of Stalin's mistakes, Dad? Can somebody please tell me the truth? Why can't you ever tell me the truth?"

"Enough!"

Dad's fist banged on top of the TV set so hard that the wire shot out from it and the spiderweb dropped from the ceiling onto the table, set for dinner.

"It's all your fault!" Dad shouted at Mom. "Admiring those traitors, those defectors. Or is it what he's learning at your Bruni's house? I warned you she's not to be trusted!" He glared at me. "Look here, son. I'll explain it to you simply."

He cleared his throat as if he was about to deliver a speech. "Under the direction of the Communist Party, the people of our mighty socialist Motherland are building a communist society with its abundant and joyous life, while the capitalist oppressors . . ."

He smacked the TV again and shouted at me, "When did you last draw a picture, I would like to know? Your new sketchbook is empty! I looked. We didn't get it for free, you know. Mother and I have to work very hard so you can develop your artistic talent!"

Dad was shouting and banging his fist on the TV and changing the subject, but he was only pretending to be angry. Really, I think he was scared. All three were. Stalin was long dead and they were still scared of him.

I laid the stamped coupon Dad was hoping for on the table. "I had no time to draw, Dad. I was too busy collecting paper."

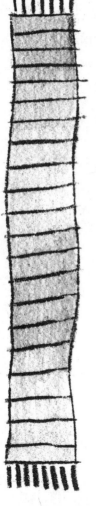

44

NEXT MORNING, GRANDMA woke me up long before the alarm rang.

"Go take him the scarf."

"What? What scarf?"

"Do I know what scarf? Scarf. He only has one. Your father rushed off in such a blitz, he forgot it."

"I have to go to school, Grandma."

"School can wait."

I looked at the window. Pitch-black outside. Snowing hard.

"Where's Mom?"

"At her lunatic place, Vaganovka. Where else would she be?"

"Dad's at work?"

"What work? He's in line. You gave him the coupon; he's in line."

"In line? How early did he leave? It's not even seven yet."

"Last night he left."

"He was standing in line all night?"

"For a book he is standing. Can you eat a book? Can you drink a book? He'll catch the death of cold for that book. Go give the scarf to your meshuggeneh father. I worry a little."

45

THE LINE TO EXCHANGE stamped coupons for a book of poems by Osip Mandelstam was so long that I could have probably read the whole book in the time it took me to find my dad in that line. The air was so thick with falling snow that everyone looked like a snowman.

Finally I saw him.

Dad must have been in a big hurry to get there, because he had forgotten more than his scarf. His overcoat, hat, and gloves were also missing. Tiny icicles sprouted from his eyebrows, and two clumps of frozen snot blocked his nostrils.

"What are you doing here, Yevgeny? You brought my scarf? How sweet of you, my dear."

He tried to wrap the scarf around his neck, but his fingers were too stiff. I tied the scarf for him.

"Thank you, Yevgeny, thank you. Much better. I'm awfully sorry for raising my voice at you last night, awfully sorry. Please forgive me, my dear."

"Why don't you go home, Dad? I'll keep your place in line."

"No, no, no! You must go to school. How are your grades? Good? I'm not surprised. With your talent."

He stumbled, swayed forward, and bumped against the back of the man standing in front of him.

"Beg your pardon, comrade!"

The comrade did not turn around. He was asleep on his feet.

"Come closer, Yevgeny. I want to tell you something."

Dad leaned into me. He was shivering and clacking his teeth.

"It's about my pencil, Yevgeny. Remember? You were stealing it to draw under the table?"

"Yes, Dad. I remember."

"After you stopped taking it from me, I thought,

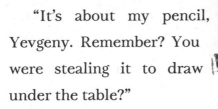

well, Comrade Yelchin, now that you have your pencil at night, you can write some brilliant rhymes."

"Rhymes? You're a poet, Dad?"

"Some poet I am. I love poetry like your mama loves ballet, but . . ." He sighed.

"I can't be a poet."

"Why, Dad? You don't have talent for it?"

"Talent? Nothing to do with talent, Yevgeny."

He was leaning into me with all his weight, blinking his snow-plastered eyelashes very fast, as if to keep from crying.

"Remember what I told you the day we went to the bathhouse? Before your Vaganovka audition?"

"About Mandelstam?"

"No, Yevgeny, about truth. To be a poet, you can't be afraid to tell the truth. That's it, Yevgeny. That simple. I'm afraid to tell the truth."

He pushed himself away from me, swayed, and leaned against the back of the comrade in front of him.

"But what about Mandelstam, Dad? 'Poetry is so respected in Russia that poets are killed for it.' Is that true?"

Dad stared at me for a moment and he nodded, a tiny little nod I could have missed if I was not looking closely.

"So, was he?" I said.

"Was he what?"

"Killed for it?"

Dad's blue lips moved, but no words came out.

"Say it, Dad. Say it so I can hear."

He nodded again and whispered, "Yes, Yevgeny, he was."

"See, Dad, you can be a poet. You just told the truth."

He smiled. "Thanks for the scarf, Yevgeny. You run to school now."

"I want to stay with you, Dad."

"Go, go. We'll read Mandelstam together tonight."

46

TWO DAYS LATER, my dad died from pneumonia at Hospital #28 on Decembrists Street.

He had made it home with the book of Mandelstam's poems, but he was too sick to read them to me. In the middle of the night, Mom sent Victor to fetch a doctor from a nearby clinic. The doctor he brought back turned out to be the mother of Yurka Semenov, one of my classmates.

"Nothing to worry about," she said. "Simple cold."

Yurka's mother was sleepy and annoyed that we made her come to our room for no reason.

Dad became delirious by morning. We could not understand what he was saying, but I thought he was reciting his favorite poems.

Victor went out to get a taxi, and we took Dad to the Hospital #28, which was overcrowded and dirty. No bed was available for my dad. He died on a cot in a hallway, with people walking by and talking in loud voices.

My classmate Yurka Semenov had nothing to do with his mother being a bad doctor, but we did not speak again, as if he felt responsible for his mother's incompetence while I felt responsible for my father's death.

On a frosty February morning, my dad was buried in the Jewish section of the Leningrad Southern Cemetery. The Soviet army contributed a military honor to the funeral because much of Dad's life was spent in the service. He reached the rank of major and was awarded the Order of Red Banner for outstanding courage on the battlefield, but when our government decided that persons of Jewish ethnicity should not be allowed to hold high military ranks, Dad was discharged.

An officer led four privates armed with AK-47s to the freshly dug grave. They fired three shots in the air. My mother fainted and missed the casket being lowered into the grave. Two men shoveled dirt into the hole. When the frozen lumps of earth clobbered the coffin's lid below the ground, I felt that someone was looking at me from behind. I turned around. A man in a shabby black coat was peeking from behind an old Jewish tombstone.

It was Blinov, our old neighbor. The KGB informer.

47

EXCEPT FOR THE SOLDIERS, everyone came home with us after the funeral. Family friends crowded our room and the hallway, talking about my dad in low voices. Our neighbors came with food and drinks for everyone. Even though Dad was just another yid to them, our neighbors had always liked him.

Nobody invited Blinov, but he showed up anyway, about an hour later, drunk.

Grandma and I were alone in the kitchen when Blinov staggered in through the front door. He still had a key.

"Don't I just know how you feel, boy," he said to me. "Your daddy . . . A fine man he was. A true communist."

We had not seen Blinov since he had left for Canada to spy on Baryshnikov. Nobody knew what had happened to him, but something must have happened, because he had aged so much, I could barely recognize him. Even his

KGB eyes—clear, cold, colorless splinters of ice—which had
scared me in the past, had become bleary and watery, as if
the ice had melted.

He wobbled toward the hallway, but Grandma
stood in his path.

"What do you want?"

"Condolences to the widow?" Blinov said.

"The widow he wants," Grandma said.
"You're drunk."

Blinov nodded, accepting.

"They kicked me out of the State
Security, Grandmother," he said. "Failed to
perform duty to the Motherland."

"I care? Go home."

"But listen, Grandmother, what could I
do? Did you see his thighs? The muscles on them? Even by
car you couldn't catch him."

"What is he talking about?" Grandma said to me.

"I think he's talking about Baryshnikov, Grandma."

Swaying, Blinov rummaged through his pockets, found
a pack of cigarettes, shook one out, and stuck it in the
corner of his mouth.

"The night after the ballet was over, a crowd of them, the

foreigners, was waiting for him outside. They had to have his signature, see? I'm in the car with the others, watching him signing his name. Right away, I knew that something was wrong. He's a smiley type, but no smile on him in that crowd. I said to the chief, 'He looks jumpy.'"

Blinov was slapping at his pockets, looking for matches. He could barely stand on his feet. The cigarette was stuck to his lower lip, bopping up and down as he spoke.

"Next, we couldn't see him anymore. Where did he go? The chief said to me, 'Go get him, idiot!' So I went. Pushed through the crowd, around the corner, and what do you know? He's running. 'Misha,' I holler, 'where are you off to?' The traitor keeps running. And how! I tried but couldn't catch him. No weapon on me, see? Not allowed. I could have shot him no problem."

He found the matches, struck one, and lit his cigarette.

"Tell the widow, Grandmother, that her friend Blinov failed to stop her Baryshnikov from defecting. For which Blinov was punished accordingly. Before we went, I was

promised a private apartment, a personal car . . . Got this instead."

He opened his mouth to show us. Half of his teeth were gone.

"I'm here secretly, see? Incognito. I'm not allowed in Leningrad. Came back to beg for my job back. Do you think they'd give it to me?"

"You need that job like a hole in your head," Grandma said. "Go now."

Blinov nodded, dropped his cigarette to the floor, squashed it with his shoe. He was halfway out when he stopped and turned around.

"That swastika on the door? Remember? 'Beat yids—save Mother Russia'? I wrote that. Not that boy your grandson beat up on. The order came from my superiors, so I did it. I swear, Grandmother, I felt bad scaring you. You're a nice old lady. I always liked you. But I had no choice, see? Got to follow the rules."

48

TWO YEARS PASSED, but still we could not get used to life without Dad. Every Sunday morning, Mom and I boarded a bus and headed to the Leningrad Southern Cemetery, where Mom laid fresh flowers on Dad's grave and spoke to him for hours.

She always began with talk of Baryshnikov.

"Misha is doing well for himself in America. Remember you were saying? You were right. Already he has danced more ballets there than in all his years at the Kirov. Are you surprised? With Misha's talent?"

While Mom looked for the handkerchief in her purse, she named all the ballets Baryshnikov was dancing in

America. Then she would wipe her tears and move on to Victor.

"You'd be so proud of your oldest. He got married. Yes, to Irina, his figure-skating partner. They are leading dancers at the Leningrad Ballet on Ice, can you imagine? We don't see them much because they're always touring foreign countries. They're allowed."

Mom would tell Dad about Victor's new private one-bedroom apartment that had a balcony, not a big balcony, but big enough to step outside for a breath of fresh air. From that balcony, Victor could see his new car parked down below.

"Who in our family ever owned a car?" Mom would say. "Nobody I know. But your oldest, he has one!"

Then Mom would tell Dad about Grandma.

"Mama is a little worse. But with her indigestion, what can we expect? A miracle? Now she talks Yiddish back to the TV. Like they understand Yiddish?"

Often while talking to Dad, Mom would smile, but there was so much pain in her smile that I had to look away.

"Yevgeny, I don't know. Tatiana Georgievna recommends he try for the Academy of Theater Arts. Maybe he can become a theater designer like her. Why not, with his artistic talent? But I worry a little. They're taking fewer Jews at colleges now. Like you said, Israel and America are stirring the pot, making it hard for us here. Some Jews can't stand it anymore and go to Israel for good, but don't you worry, darling—we'll never leave you behind."

Next, I would take a stroll among the Jewish graves. Mom needed time alone to talk to Dad about herself.

49

IT WAS ON ONE of those long bus trips to the Leningrad Southern Cemetery that I asked Mom about my grandfather again. What happened to him? Was he really arrested?

"Please don't ask me, honey. Your father didn't want you kids to know."

"But why, Mom?"

She looked away from me and stared through the window. Huge portraits of our aging leaders, propped up along the side of the road, glared at us as we passed.

"Where we live, Yevgeny," Mom said, "it's safer that way, you know?"

"No, I don't know, Mom. I don't. Why does it make it safer not to know what happened to your own grandfather?"

Did I raise my voice at her? Maybe I did because a man sitting in front of us got up and moved away. The bus driver was staring at me in the rearview mirror. Mom, her eyes swelled with tears, was digging into her purse for a handkerchief.

"I'm sorry, Mom. Please don't be upset. I'll never ask you again—I promise."

And I kept my promise. I never asked her again. I never found out what happened to my grandfather. Even our photo album soon disappeared, and I never saw those cut-up family photos again. Grandma must have hidden it somewhere.

Our past—my family's past as well as the past of my country—had so many terrible secrets that my questions caused nothing but fear in people I loved. I saw that fear in the eyes of my dad, and my mom, and my grandma, but also in the eyes of strangers I passed in the streets every day. Our Soviet citizens' eyes were often half-shut and glossed over, as if they would rather stare inside their frightened selves than at the menacing world outside.

But there were also other eyes in Leningrad. Eyes that shone with curiosity and passion, eyes starved for something more than our drab existence. I had seen such eyes in lines waiting for Baryshnikov to dance, and I had seen such eyes in our libraries, our theaters, our museums, and our concert halls.

Those curious and passionate eyes made me happy. Yes, in spite of everything, I was happy. Our Soviet force of gravity was already losing its hold on me. I was eager and impatient to fly. Our past lay hidden in darkness, but my future seemed dazzlingly bright.

QUESTIONS TO CONSIDER

1. *The Genius Under the Table* is an intriguing title. What did you think the book would be about?

2. Did you know the term *Iron Curtain* before you read this book? What did you learn about life behind the Iron Curtain from this book?

3. This is a fictionalized memoir; in other words, it is about the young Eugene (Yevgeny) Yelchin's life, but it is not a strict account. What do you think he omitted? Is there anything you would like to know more about?

4. Opposite the title page are pictures of the people in Yevgeny's family set up like a photo album: Mom, Dad, Grandma, Grandpa, brother Victor, and Yevgeny himself. But the grandpa picture has had the face cut out. Why would someone have done that?

5. What does Yevgeny think about Americans and America? From where does he get his impressions? Do you think they are accurate?

6. Children are generally very curious, and Yevgeny is no exception, but his parents tell him that asking questions is considered not patriotic. What do they mean by that?

7. On page 95, Yevgeny's father says, "You can never be a great poet, Yevgeny, if you're afraid to tell the truth. But truth is a dangerous thing. Most people don't like it." What do you think he means by this?

8. In chapter 39 (pages 157–160), Yevgeny explains that he has realized that there are three kinds of Russian artists: those who defect so they can continue painting the way they want; those who stay and continue to paint the way they want, but may be arrested or even killed; and those who stay and learn to paint by the rules. Which path do you think you would choose?

Adapted from the discussion guide prepared by Grace Worcester for Candlewick Press